# About Power

# Wisdom Editions

Minneapolis

First Edition August 2024
*About Power: How to Democratize Electricity Now.*
Copyright © 2024 by George W. Crocker. All rights reserved.

10 9 8 7 6 5 4 3 2 1

ISBN: 978-1-962834-21-6

Cover and book design by Gary Lindberg

# About Power

How to Democratize Electricity Now

George W. Crocker

Wisdom
Editions

Minneapolis

"The measurement of a man is what he does with power."

–Plato, The Republic

"The white man knows how to make everything, but he does not know how to distribute anything."

–Tatanka Iyotaka 1890 (Sitting Bull)

# Table of Contents

# Introduction / Chapter 1

When I was growing up in the 1950s and '60s, the thinking about the word "apocalypse" had a slightly different twist to it than it has today. Not that behavior giving rise to such thinking has improved much, because it has not, and the threat of thermonuclear annihilation keeps the Doomsday Clock set perilously close to midnight. While many aspects of the Cold War remain, and some are heating up, the twist is that back then, a reality driven by Climate Chaos was scarcely imagined and still decades in the future. Nuclear Winter, maybe, but not global warming.

Such a future is now upon us, though, and if the warring and the chaos are not enough for you, there's a cascade of natural and concocted germs and viruses running amok. Dioxins, PFAS, radionuclides, CFCs, plastics, acidic and other environmental contaminants are infesting all earthly biological genomes and threatening sterility prior to agonizing death. Earth's sixth or seventh mass extinction event, depending on whether the first one counts, is well underway. Fascism driven by misinformation, bigotry and perceptions of deprivation, real and imagined, is on the rise, and regardless of how much root it takes here or elsewhere on the planet, human decision-making processes need rapid, drastic improvement in order to deal with the coming Real Live Planetary Ecological Horror Show, and who knows which things artificial intelligence will make better, and which things it will make worse. What to do, what to do.

1

Well, for starters, one can take solace in the fact that clever humans are clever enough to now look back at the very beginning of time and space, and gaze upon, with a growing degree of comprehension, the awesome splendor and vastness of our Universe. If nothing else, such observation can provide a bit of perspective on the magnitude and the folly of our troubles here on Earth. But our ability to make such observation also creates a hope, maybe, that human cleverness can mature into an intelligence that is able to recognize how to correct the social and economic structures that already are collapsing around us, structures that activated, clever, intelligent, and decent humans can reconstruct and imbue with human dignity and perhaps even a bit of economic democracy. Maybe.

I have struggled with aspects of this hope since I was a child. "Why are people like this?" I remember wondering in 1958 as I shot hoops in the gym while my fifth grade classmates in Lake Elmo cowered beneath their desks, as if they were actually hiding from The Bomb. I got to go shoot hoops because my parents were a little different. Dad took his Christianity seriously and believed that when Jesus preached his Sermon on the Mount, it was in fact meant to be instructive. For that, Dad got yelled at by his preacher where he went for counseling and got kicked out of his Congregationalist Church for being a coward. But he stuck to his guns, so to speak, got classified as a Conscientious Objector by the Selective Service System during World War II, and spent the war years in a Civilian Public Service camp near Missoula, Montana, jumping out of airplanes to put out forest fires. Mom was the camp nurse, one of two or three women in a camp of 400 young men, and Dad brought her home with him after the war. So when Mom and Dad heard about the "duck & cover" program, they had words with the School District Superintendent, and when my classmates had to curl up under their desks, I got to go shoot hoops.

Well, humans *are* like that, I realized as my country required me to participate in its war mongering less than a decade later. My options were forced and difficult, as they were for all young men who came of age in that time, but it turned out that choosing the "human dignity" side of things made for some interesting adventures. And so my stories began as I confronted the war machine that the United Stated government was using in its tragically misguided attempt to prevent the "domino effect" in Southeast Asia. I joined the Anti-war Movement, organized resistance to the draft and against the war, and got sentenced to four years in a federal penitentiary for refusing to comply with General Hershey's orders. I served eighteen months at the federal prison in Milan, Michigan.

While I remember these and my other adventures with a sense of satisfaction, for obvious reasons I still find the "hope" part challenging. But then, as I write about my stories and the things I have learned over decades of confronting and cajoling and sometimes directing the behavior of electric utilities, it seems that the whole concept of hopefulness takes a spin through some weird kaleidoscope and the stories themselves offer a way forward because after all, the main reason to share them is because younger people where I work, still, sort of, on energy issues, have urgently and repeatedly encouraged me to do so. They want their stories. They want to know why energy management, energy policy and so much of the rest of it, is so utterly and absurdly misguided. Here is a hint: it has to do with incentives. We tend to get the behavior we reward, and as a society, we reward a lot of horrific behavior that requires confrontation.

When the time comes for me to share my stories about activities in which I did my best to relate with decency to circumstances that confronted me, and that I chose to confront, perhaps they will offer insight as to why so much is so warped, and what to do about it. Plus, sometimes the jokes are funny. But for now, the stories will mostly have to wait. Urgent action to curb escalating destruction from Climate Chaos is needed now, and the publisher of my stories has the notion that the knowledge I gained while creating them will be helpful guidance for the required urgent actions. I hope he's right. We'll see.

For now, think about the hint. Then, let's say that a major cause of Climate Chaos is gasses that are released into the atmosphere by fossil fuel combustion, and that the more fossil fuel combustion there is, the greater is the contribution of fossil fuel combustion gasses to Climate Chaos, and the more chaotic things become. On April 10, 2024, the United Nations climate chief said that humans have two years left "to save the world." He went on to talk about the required shift in technologies and the finances that need to get behind such a massive transformation. But if it seems so clear that reducing fossil fuel combustion gasses to the atmosphere is a vital part of the strategy to reduce the damage Climate Chaos causes, why, then, does the financial health of monopolistic power companies improve when they sell more electricity and spew more carbon dioxide into the atmosphere? This is absolutely backward! Why do our regulatory institutions insist on rewarding behavior that is actively eroding our ecological foundation?

So, something to do about it would be to change power company incentive structures to reward energy efficiency, instead of energy consumption. Electric utility regulation could be reformed, for example, so that power companies sell energy services rather than selling kilowatt hours as a commodity, and then the power company would be rewarded for providing those services as efficiently as possible. We do it backward. If things were not backward, power companies would make more money and have greater financial health as they delivered more service while consumers used less electricity. Correcting this regulatory flaw alone would eliminate most, if not all $CO_2$ dumped into the atmosphere by US electric utilities, which amounts to a third of all US emissions, or something over 1,500 million metric tons per year in 2022. This correction alone would reduce global $CO_2$ emissions by almost three percent, enough to start reversing the global trend of annual $CO_2$ emissions increases. Making this correction is difficult not just because large numbers of powerful people make lots of money by doing it backward, but also in significant part because so many electric utility customers are functionally illiterate when it comes to energy management. How many consumers understand the difference between a megawatt and a kilo-watt-hour, for instance? Conversely, knowledge is power.

How transmission infrastructure gets developed provides a glaring example, not of backward energy management, but of managing it upside down. No doubt you have heard ignorant, foolish, or self-serving people purport that hundreds of billions of dollars' worth of new high-voltage transmission infrastructure is desperately needed to develop enough renewable energy to make a difference environmentally, and that we have to make the commitment for that new transmission now due to the climate emergency and the long lead times required for powerline construction. This all may be true, but only if you want top down transmission development, and what you want sometime five or ten years from now, is a relatively few large corporations owning massive wind and solar farms located at remote locations, mostly somewhere on the Great Plains. With such a development scenario, wind and solar energy resources become commodities that get extracted for exclusive private profit, should we get that far, while the consuming public pays for the extraction by purchasing infrastructure, the high-voltage transmission lines, needed to deliver the power to load centers. With the UN climate chief saying we've got two years, why would we want to choose the five to ten year option?

But it is also possible, and *much* cheaper and quicker, to strategically size new wind and solar installations, perhaps along with battery storage, and connect them to the grid on the lower-voltage side of virtually *every load-serving substation transformer in the nation,* without requiring *any* new high-voltage transmission. The strategic sizing causes all the power from the new renewable generators to be consumed by customers served by a specific substation or set of substations serving that particular neighborhood. No power would ever flow back into the higher voltage system, which is why no new transmission would be needed. In Minnesota alone, this type of "bottom up" approach amounts to well over 8,000 MW of new wind and solar generation that could be distributed and disbursed around the state, with no need for new power lines. (For comparison, roughly 18,600 MW of installed generation capacity served Minnesota loads in 2022.) Then, over time, even when new loads come online, the lower-voltage distribution network could be strategically enhanced as needed to accommodate additional generation capacity to serve the local area and its neighboring areas, still without the need for any new high-voltage transmission.

One added benefit of this "bottom up" approach is that it makes our energy system much more robust and resilient because each neighborhood contributes significantly to the production of the power it requires, and each neighborhood is interconnected to adjacent neighborhoods as well as the higher voltage grid for added security. Another is that it readily lends itself to ownership within the community being served. The power that serves the community also becomes an economic engine that would enhance the financial well-being of the community producing and consuming the power. Economic democracy. Of course, that is also the problem, because then the market share of monopoly power companies would rapidly evaporate, and those who benefit economically from the status quo would rather continue with the ecological horror show than lose market share. The important point is that we *do* have options.

On the demand side of delivering electric utility services, we will show how things got backward by rewarding power companies for increasing electrical energy production while energy consumption increases, instead of rewarding energy efficiency. On the supply side, we will show how things got upside down by accommodating large, private, remote renewable energy projects that require expensive, publicly funded new high-voltage transmission infrastructure, rather than first deploying strategically sized new renewable generation facilities within the footprint of load-serving substations that requires *no* new transmission, and then incrementally enhancing lower-voltage transmission infrastructure to accommodate the next deployment of strategically sized generation, and so on, from the bottom up, in an iterative process.

This upside down and backwardness approach to power that we have, is driving society headlong into Climate Chaos and is a fundamental cause of major social inequities and economic disparities. Also, it quite naturally leads to elemental mischaracterizations of basic terms and definitions that are used to describe the system that delivers to us our electric utility services. For instance, what do we mean when we say "baseload?" Ask any electric utility manager or engineer, or regulator, or politician who knows the difference between a kilowatt-hour and a megawatt, or virtually any activist person attempting to inject a bit of sanity into the electric utility system, and they will tell you that "baseload" refers to the electrical load that is online 24/7, even during nighttime hours when electrical consumption is at the lowest part of the load duration curve. Baseload power plants, therefore, are the very large coal and nuclear electric generation facilities that want to be online all the time except for maintenance and refueling, because they are intended to serve this continuous base load as cheaply as possible.

Once we make it out of the central station paradigm, however, and fully enter the Modern Era of electric utility services, should civil society, such as it is, make it that far, "baseload" will have quite a different meaning. Rather than being this massive, ubiquitous, undifferentiated load served by massive, remote central station powerplants, "baseload" will be defined as the discrete, unique load that is the minimum load within the footprint of each load-serving substation or group of interconnected substations that directly serve electric consumers within the footprint. In the Modern Era, "baseload" will therefore define, substation by load-serving substation, the amount of electrical generation capacity that can be deployed within the footprint of each load-serving substation without requiring any new transmission infrastructure.

Following this logic, "intermediate loads" will be all the discrete electric loads within the footprint of each load-serving substation that are above each substation footprint's baseload. Dispersed and distributed generation capacity brought online to serve intermediate loads may get curtailed from time to time due to transmission constraints, but these will be fluid situations as transmission systems get enhanced, iteration by iteration, from lower to higher voltages, to accommodate new increments of strategically sized and located renewable generation. As the energy transition unfolds, dispersed and distributed generation and iterative transmission enhancements will systematically back out old-paradigm central station machines. When the energy transition is complete, base and intermediate loads will be served by dispersed and distributed renewable generation plus battery storage capacity, and "peak loads," instead of referring to electric consumption on the hottest and the coldest days of the year, will designate the largest and most dense of industrial loads that may still require central station generators.

The key to accomplishing corrective action, of course, is intelligent involvement. Individually, and collectively as possible, so long as it's decent. Since 1982, my involvement centered on the agenda my lovely wife Lea and I constructed for the North American Water Office (NAWO), a non-profit we co-founded in the wake of the First Battle of America's Energy War and the Black Hills Survival Gathering. We pursued that agenda until 2010 or so, and then I got done in, so to speak, by very specific lying and cheating over how to analyze the need for transmission infrastructure enhancements, on the part of public and private electric utility personnel, their regulators and their hired help. They had to lie and cheat in order to preserve the thievery enabled by monopoly structures of the electric utility industry. It did me in, and then I went to my very own little private version of hell.

During my time there, I spent many of my waking hours simply ranting as the dog walked me through the woods. During that time, Lea said the garden was cleaner than it had ever been before. I was saved, so to speak, by intergenerational wealth. Mom and Dad weren't rich, but they worked hard, Dad as a union carpenter and Mom as a nurse. Dad built the house we live in still. We held his memorial service on the day Chernobyl blew up. Lea and I moved our family back home in 1987, where Mom had her own walk-out basement apartment, and which is why, over twenty years later, I had a woods to walk through while I ranted.

It took me several years to realize that done in or not, I was actually very close to Heaven, what with the garden and the woods and my family and all, and that the only death was that of my direct professional relationship with a gang of lying, cheating, cut-throat thieves. I could no longer stand to be in their presence. When I tried, a furious rage inside me boiled up, demanding a response to their ignominious corruption that would not allow me to remain decent. So I left, and I ranted.

There I was, professionally out of it, but living next to Heaven, and with a federally recognized nonprofit to run. NAWO somehow needed new blood, I eventually realized, and so I asked a young twenty-something Timothy if he would care to meet with myself and Louis, who has been with NAWO for decades, to see what interest he might have in joining our Board of Directors. Young as he was, Timothy had already established a name for himself through his involvement with energy issues before state agencies and the state legislature, which is why we asked him, and he agreed to meet. This was in November 2011. As we talked about the work that needed doing, the franchise agreements that the City of Minneapolis had with the gas and electric utilities serving Minneapolis customers entered the discussion.

Franchise Agreements are contracts that many cities have with the gas and electric utilities that serve customers within their city limits. A franchise agreement contract specifies the terms and conditions whereby the utilities are given the exclusive right to provide utility services in the city, and in exchange for being allowed to use city property for utility infrastructure like power poles and gas pipelines, the utility pays the city a big chunk of cash. Between CenterPoint Energy and Xcel Energy, that chunk of cash amounts to somewhere around $30 million per year flowing into the coffers of the City of Minneapolis. Historically, most franchise agreements, including those between Minneapolis and Xcel and CenterPoint, were for twenty years. The contracts Minneapolis had with CenterPoint Energy on the gas side, and Xcel Energy for electricity, were coming up for renewal in 2014.

Back in 1994 I knew that Minneapolis was again making a bad deal with CenterPoint and Northern States Power Co. (before it became Xcel Energy), but back then, there was no effective opportunity to engage the matter, and besides, I was thoroughly occupied with the ongoing Prairie Island nuclear waste fight that was now six years old, and that we had finally gotten to the Minnesota Legislature. By the time we had our meeting with Timothy in 2011, twenty years had not yet quite passed, and after our discussion, we decided that rather than dealing with North American Water Office issues, we would find out if there was any activity with which we could engage around the negotiations to renew the franchise agreements. So the next day I called Cam Gordon's office. Cam was a member of the Minneapolis City Council. There are thirteen members on the Minneapolis City Council, and twelve of them were formally affiliated with the Minnesota Democratic Farmer Labor Party, the DFL. The thirteenth was Cam, and Cam was a Green.

Robin, Cam's Chief of Staff, answered the phone. "Hello," I said and introduced myself. "What's going on with the franchise agreement?" I asked, "Is anybody doing anything about that?"

"Where have you been?" responded Robin, and my dead professional life entered a whole new set of dimensions.

Both Timothy and Robin knew a fine assortment of younger people who understood, at least in broad outlines, the ecological calamity lurking on the horizon. These younger people fully understood that meager state requirements for energy conservation and renewable energy were nowhere near sufficient to actually make a difference, and they wanted to do something about it. Cam was set and ready, with the resources of his public office available for our campaign, and we began to plot. John, with the Institute for Local Self-Reliance (ILSR) immediately joined the fray and brought with him the considerable resources, both in terms of time and expertise, that he and ILSR had to offer. The Minnesota Public Interest Research Group (MPIRG), a grassroots, non-partisan, non-profit student-directed organization that engages the community to take collective action in the public interest throughout the state, got involved.

Lee was on the case with fervent intensity from the beginning, as was Marcus with his invaluable political analysis and insightful judgment regarding when and who to engage, and how to engage them. Alice, who worked to support our effort from its beginning, joined the team a few years later and has been instilling a bit of fear and constructive uncertainty, along with a lot of respect, in an assortment of utility managers and bureaucrats ever since. We raised a little money and hired Dylan as our staff to help keep us focused and coordinated.

We organized ourselves as Minneapolis Energy Options with the intent of presenting Minneapolis voters with a choice: either continue meekly down the road to doom with Xcel and CenterPoint, or else vote to take away their franchise and instead create a new municipal power authority. Our intent was to put the question on the city election ballot in 2013. We wanted a power company that would fight global warming with the combined power of all Minneapolis energy consumers. We wanted to rectify disparities regarding how utility services get delivered to low-income city residents compared to wealthier neighborhoods, and to stop these two corporations from profiteering at the expense of Minneapolis energy consumers.

During the first couple years of this campaign, and until we could stand up on our own, we were able to use offices at city hall that Cam made available to us, to hold our meetings and plan our actions. We organized everything from large events to neighborhood gatherings to educate and inform city voters and each other about what was wrong with the status quo, and what the options were for those who wanted to work toward correcting the problems.

Of course, throughout this campaign we knew that our chances of actually kicking Xcel and CenterPoint out of Minneapolis were a little less than zero because of the "poison pill" in Minnesota statutes that decades ago, power companies got passed through the legislature to protect their earnings as well as their investments. We will examine why this is in due course, but for now suffice it to say that according to MN Stat. 216B.45, if a municipality terminates the franchise agreement it has with a utility, the municipality must pay the utility not only fair market value for all the infrastructure owned by the utility that is used to serve energy customers in the municipality, but also, the municipality must pay the loss of revenue to the utility that the utility would make if it were not being bought out. So, obviously, we need to change that state law before enlightened and informed consumers will have the power to directly hold power companies accountable.

Accountability takes many forms, however, and our Minneapolis Energy Options campaign was informing a whole lot of Minneapolis residents about the unfortunate realities attached to their energy situation, including the "poison pill," and a very large majority were not pleased. Xcel Energy and CenterPoint began hearing about the failings and unfairness of their agreement with the city, and the volume of those communications was steadily increasing as our campaign grew. The utilities responded with a PR campaign of their own, which was pretty easy for them, as all they had to do was include their propaganda in the envelope along with their monthly energy bills. Then we knew that we had struck a nerve.

Maybe we could not actually municipalize utility services in Minneapolis, but it appeared that we had at least a chance of getting the matter put on the ballot. As this reality unfolded, it began to dawn on CenterPoint and Xcel Energy that fighting Minneapolis Energy Options over a ballot initiative in which they were the obvious bad guys, would cost them a whole lot of money. It would probably be cheaper, they began to realize, if instead they were to offer to negotiate terms and conditions of new franchise agreements, and that's what they did.

But negotiations were different this time. If CenterPoint and Xcel were to decide to try the "We Say So" approach to the negotiations, Minneapolis Energy Options would resume campaigning on the ballot initiative. The utilities did not want that, and so, for the first time in recorded history, franchise agreement negotiations consisted of something other than haggling over what the compensation number would be for the next twenty years.

The City Council was well motivated. On August 13, 2013, it passed Resolution 2013R-353 that adopted a framework for reaching City of Minneapolis energy goals. The resolution did "Whereas" ten times and "Be it Resolved and Further Resolved" six times, including calling for the creation of a formal city/utility partnership. The result of the ensuing negotiations gave us hope that maybe there is a chance of improving energy management significantly and quickly, because the City of Minneapolis, CenterPoint, and Xcel Energy actually did create the nation's first formal city/utility energy management partnership, the Minneapolis Clean Energy Partnership. The Obama White House publicly recognized this achievement, and the Pope, who was becoming increasingly alarmed as Climate Chaos gained more traction, invited Minneapolis Mayor Betsy Hodges to the Vatican so he could point to Minneapolis as an example of how communities could begin to work in the right direction. Further, in recognition of the reality that the energy industry is in a transition period, instead of a twenty year contract, the city could now opt to renegotiate any time after the first four years.

The partnership has resulted in a surge of local solar energy projects owned cooperatively by local residents and installed by companies like Cooperative Energy Futures, of which Timothy is the General Manager, and residential solar installations are becoming more routine. On the other hand, Xcel is finding creative ways to add red tape to the development of renewable energy projects in Minneapolis that it does not own, and doing things like cutting the price it pays for energy purchased from such projects, and increasing fees attached to interconnection agreements. CenterPoint, meanwhile, is slow-walking or outright blocking regulatory reform that would allow consumers to pay for energy efficiency improvements over time with the value of the energy they save. The struggle continues. More information about both the Minneapolis Clean Energy Partnership, Cooperative Energy Futures and Community Power is readily available online.

My involvement with the younger people working to dramatically improve energy management in Minneapolis inspired me to write my stories, and to offer them such guidance as I am able. Perhaps this brilliant team that we have put together, and their colleagues across the nation and the world will be able to correct the flaws that must be corrected if the worst of an apocalyptic future is to be avoided. Because of their brilliance, and their knowledge of the flaws that need correcting, there is good reason to conclude that generations to come will know their history and understand how the institutions that provide their goods and services can do so decently. But the younger people I am working with suffer no illusions. They regularly engage in discussion about how to live in a postapocalyptic world. In the Fall of 2023, I helped a crew of them gather acorns. It was a mast year, in which a single large oak tree can drop more than 10,000 acorns filled with protein, if you know how to process acorns. It might be good to learn how to do that in times to come.

With that in mind, it must be acknowledged that the people of my generation, the Boomers, will mostly get away with squandering huge opportunity to form a more perfect union, so to speak, while consuming vast wealth wastefully, and with gusto. Hence our existential challenges. Boomers will probably go down in history as the generation that took the most and gave the least, and for that, I am profoundly sorry. But know this: if/when humans get energy management right, humans will have the ability to do everything that decently needs doing, because we'll have the power we need to do it.

# Chapter 2
## Situation

The reason for this book is that my publisher told me I had to write it before he would consider all the stories I have already written about selected circumstances I have encountered in my time, which impart, more or less, some of the same information, but are a little more spontaneous and they have more jokes.

The other reason for this book is to instigate civil actions in which humans must engage if we are to survive the storm. It is upon us, it will continue to intensify for decades to come, it is accelerated by warring and bigotry and ignorant resource management, and we need a bigger movement to address it. We need a movement that will correct the behavior of human institutions that have caused this storm, and that have proven themselves to be unable to correct behaviors that propel humanity toward multidimensional catastrophe. Much of the work that needs doing to appropriately reverse these trends, from environmental protection to health care to gainful employment and gun safety, and on to a large number of other vital fronts, is already being done. Some of it is done in isolation, some is organized a bit and some is organized a lot. But ecological foundations continue eroding, and the warring and the exploitations continue while the storm expands in size and fury. So human and natural resource management practices face an existential choice: improve dramatically and quickly, or the structures that provide our goods and services will disintegrate. In short, we need a movement that can guide humanity toward human and natural resource management that allows human society to bequeath human society to posterity.

This movement needs to change how vegetable and mineral resources get extracted from the Earth and distributed to the consuming public. It needs to change how wastes from production processes get managed for virtually every waste stream that exists. This movement must figure out how to stop the warring. It needs to institutionalize adequate and universal health care. It needs to eliminate racial, gender and other discriminations. It needs to promote freedom of thought and expression and creativity and art. We need a movement that strives toward Utopia in all its aspects and glory, and if we strive for anything less, the foundations of civilization, such as it is, will continue crumbling until they collapse.

For all I know, the treatises that define a proper way of providing universal health care have already been written. Likewise for proper management of thousands of waste streams, and resource extractions, and the re-discovering of non-profit community media, and much of the rest of it. These treatises may have been written, but if so, they have not been implemented, or not enough of them, otherwise our foundations would not still be crumbling at an accelerating pace. Specifications for proper management of many additional processes and procedures have not even been written yet. What is the best way to manage PFAS? Or microplastics, for example? One sector that is a work in progress has to do with how electric utility services get delivered, and this book devotes its attention in that direction because I have worked most of my life to improve that delivery. But energy management corrections that need to happen, and that this book calls for, have likewise not been implemented because doing so would interfere with corporate earnings and the monopoly market share of the companies that dominate the industry. That's why we need a movement.

Obviously, I have no particular expertise regarding what precisely are the proper management systems for the vast majority of human and natural resource processes and procedures that need to be revisioned. But my life has been significantly influenced by the warring, and I know a bit about movement building. This part of my education began just out of high school when I joined the resistance to the American War in Southeast Asia which eventually, along with the resolute and tenacious endurance of the Vietnamese people, became strong enough to deprive the war machine of the cannon-fodder it needed to continue. Then, eventually, this war that was so necessary to protect America from communism and preserve our "sphere of influence" ended, and now, when someone talks about "south of the border" as to where cheap labor is available, they are more likely to be talking about US multinational corporations going south from China than from the US to Mexico. What does this tell us about the value of the lives ruined and wasted because of that war?

This much is clear: the warring must stop. Warring is an accelerant to the Climate Chaos that is already burning down our house. Whether it's Ukrainians fighting for their right to exist against a fascistic egomaniac, or ancient tribal rivalries in Africa, or Zionistic zealots intent on genocide (so much for "never again") against the people of Palestine displaced by the Nakba in 1948, or wherever, the only difference between those responsible for the warring going on right now and a crazed arsonist dancing in the flames while pouring gasoline on the fire burning down his house is that the warring is on a larger scale. The warring must come to an end, or the rest of it will not much matter.

That requires a movement, but the prospects are dim. At this writing, as young people on college and university campuses across the US cry out for provoked Zionists to end their horrific genocide against provoked Palestinians, the response of Academic Management in the US is to call out the cops against the kids, bust them and kick them out of school. What have we learned since Kent State? Nevertheless, we need a movement large enough and strong enough and well enough organized so that where the warring is, the movement is capable of sending a mass of humanity to the battlefield, and that this mass of humanity is large enough and with the discipline to put a stop to it. The movement needs a functional United Nations. Either that, or we watch our house burn down with all the children and the pets inside.

With brilliant if dubious optimism, I presume that we can stop the arsonists, and so I carry on with my writing.

After the war in Southeast Asia, my education in movement building continued as I participated in the Upper Midwest Food Coop Wars in the mid-70s, and then it went further when I joined the First Battle of America's Energy War in 1977. From then on, my career centered on intervening in a wide variety of electric utility decision-making proceedings. My ability to participate meaningfully, and sometimes with success, in these proceedings often depended on my ability to help organize and coordinate the focused participation of large numbers of people over extended periods of time.

It also depended upon not making mistakes. I needed to learn a lot about how electric utility systems are managed and regulated, and I needed to learn quickly. This was decades before any formal higher education curricula about environmental impacts of producing electricity had even been thought about, and there was no place you could go to sign up and learn about the relative costs and benefits of delivering energy services one way or another. It was learning by doing, and obviously, when participating in formal decision-making proceedings with or without formal training, there is little margin for error. If you err, you lose. If you err, and you are only in the proceeding because you injected yourself into it, and you are without formal training, you lose legitimacy in a flash. If you have no legitimacy as a participant in a decision-making process, you should probably go do something else.

Fortunately, common sense and a general idea of what the public interest actually was, went a long way toward being credible in these venues, despite my lack of formal credentials. Of course, it did not hurt that with the proper analytical perspective, the self-serving behavior of utility managers and regulators alike often became as obvious as it was demonstrably destructive, if one were forced to actually look at it, which I made them do from time to time. When that happened, it did not hurt my reputation. Humor, even if it was often caustic, also helped. But because of my participation, I know multiple aspects of electric utility management and regulation that are foul and terribly misguided, and I also know what needs to be done to enable electric utility services to get delivered decently, that is, cleanly, locally, efficiently, affordably and reliably. Let's make that CLEAR.

In the wake of the West Central Minnesota powerline fight in the 1970s and 1980s, my future wife Lea and I, along with Wendel, a physics professor from Gustavus Adolphus College in St. Peter, Minnesota, formed TKO to oppose an 800 MW coal power plant called Sherco 3. TKO was The Kilowatt Organization and our letterhead read, "You Megawatt, We Kilowatt." During that intervention, TKO produced evidence that embarrassed the Minnesota Pollution Control Agency and the Minnesota Department of Health to begin issuing the state's first fish consumption advisories. We documented how mercury emitted into the atmosphere from coal fires ended up on soil and sediment where it gets methylated by bacteria and migrates to lakes and rivers where fish absorb it, and then it gets concentrated in predator fish like Northern and Walleye Pike. These are prime game fish for tourists, but they are also a traditional dietary source of protein for Indigenous Peoples, and now we are into environmental racism. Once state agencies started looking at fish contamination, they also found the dioxins and PCBs and the rest of it, and then everyone who bought a fishing license also got a little booklet that told them what they were eating. Assuming they could catch a fish. During this proceeding, TKO also introduced the Minnesota electric utility crowd to "end use analysis," about which you will learn more in due course.

Lea and I co-founded the North American Water Office as a 501(c)3 federally recognized nonprofit organization in 1982. Check out our website (www.nawo.org) if you are interested. We needed this organizational structure in order to engage with public decision-making regarding the electric utility industry on a full-time basis. Our first intervention as NAWO was to Stop Acid Rain.

Acid rain was a very big deal in the early and mid-80's. Buildings and bridges were dissolving in the acids, and so were the Adirondack Mountains. Rates of human respiratory infections and asthma were accelerated. Highly acidic early spring meltwater flowing into streams and lakes was killing entire year-classes of certain fish species. Fried the fry, so to speak. Acid sensitive lakes, those perched on bedrock in higher elevations, like in Minnesota's Boundary Waters Canoe Area, were verging toward sterility. Trees died from the top down, and forest dieback was ubiquitous and obvious in conifer forests from Minnesota to the East Coast if you knew enough to recognize it for what it was. Northern Europe got hit hard.

Uncontrolled Sulfur dioxide and Nitrogen oxide emissions from coal-fired power plants and metal smelters, and from oil refineries, were causing the destruction. But identifying individual point sources, or company fleets of point sources for acid deposition that occurs at some distant area or region after tall smokestacks have thoroughly stirred atmospheric pools of contamination is more speculative. This was particularly true in the early 1980s, which made it easy back then for individual polluters to make more money as they did a better job of denying culpability for the messes they were making. No one could prove who was responsible for what. For this reason, plus the fact that pollution control equipment to remove the acids from stack gasses is expensive, state and federal legislatures were paralyzed by industry lobbyists all pointing fingers elsewhere while the destruction escalated.

In 1982, the Minnesota Legislature, sensitized to energy issues by the recent powerline fight and intent on protecting its tourism industry, passed the nation's first law to stop acidification, the Acid Deposition Control Act. The administrative proceeding to set an acid deposition standard and to establish pollution control requirements would not commence until early 1986. But in the meanwhile, NAWO went to work and identified all 507 individual point sources of sulfur dioxide emissions in North America greater than 10,000 tons per year. We published detailed specifics about each of them in a document entitled

"SO2 Point Source Directory." We put all 507 of them, all nicely color coded, on a big map of North America that was the centerpiece of a convention-style display that also illustrated destruction caused by acidification, and strategies to solve the problem that included pollution control equipment, renewable energy and energy efficiency improvements.

By 1984, acidification was bad enough across the country that it became an issue in the US presidential campaign, at least on the Democratic Party side of things. So, a bunch of large environmental organizations got together and organized a big Acid Rain Conference in Manchester, just ahead of the New Hampshire Presidential Primary. Everybody who was anybody was there, wringing their hands over what to do, what to do. We set up our display. Everybody who was anybody came by and took a look and nodded sagely while pointing fingers to the dots on our big map, and now that the sources of the problem were so clearly identified, the discussion as to what to do about it finally began to get serious.

While the discussion at the federal level was finally underway, back in Minnesota, NAWO joined the administrative proceeding that would determine the state's acid deposition standard and control plan. The power companies argued for a standard around twenty kg. of Sulfur deposition per hectare per year, in which case they would meet the standard and be required to do nothing in terms of cleaning themselves up. State agencies, the Pollution Control Agency and the Department of Natural Resources, argued for eleven kg/ha/yr., and NAWO along with a separate environmental coalition, argued for a standard of seven.

In the course of the proceeding, the power companies put an expert witness, Dr. Krause from Germany, on the witness stand. At the time, amid much consternation, Germany was trying vainly to protect its national treasure, the Black Forest, from a slow death by acid. This expert therefore was afforded considerable credibility as he traveled the globe to argue that acidification processes were so complicated and complex that there was really nothing to be done about it. He testified

21

that he had identified 157 separate acidification processes all inter-acting with each other, and that with such a convoluted admixture, it would be impossible to tell if anything power companies were ordered to do would make any discernible difference, so it would be imprudent to order them to do anything.

When it came to be my time to cross-examine Dr. Krause, I asked him if it was true that all his 157 acidification processes could be boiled down into the proposition that acidification is a result of either a complex array of naturally occurring phenomena, or else it is due to anthropogenic activity. Well, yes, that's true, Dr. Krause acknowledged after putting up a fight, and then, under my cross-examination, he agreed that anthropogenic activities were to blame. Unprompted, he went further and testified that anything that reduced the need to burn would be an improvement.

With this information provided by the power company witness on the record, when it became time for NAWO to put on its case, I submitted evidence that, for the first time at least in North America, presented energy efficiency improvements as part of a pollution control strategy. For one example, I documented how an energy efficient light bulb is also a pollution control device. This was way before LEDs, so my testimony compared a single screw-in fluorescent light bulb, the Philips SL18, to a string of ten seventy-five watt incandescent bulbs that would be needed to last the same 7,500 hours. I showed how during that time, the SL18 would save $13 in electricity and bulb replacement costs, while reducing acid rain emissions by 16.7 pounds.

In the summer of 1986, Minnesota adopted the nation's first Acid Deposition Standard, at a relatively protective eleven kg/ha/yr. of wet sulfate, and, while recognizing that it had no authority over emissions from plants outside the state, Minnesota power companies were ordered to install the pollution control equipment needed to keep Minnesota facilities from contributing to violations. Energy efficiency improvements were also formally recognized as a component of the pollution control strategy a power company could adopt. The fact that

Minnesota acted, even though most of the pollution causing problems in Minnesota came from the Ohio River Valley and up from Texas, demonstrated to the nation that individual states could take protective action even though the federal government had done nothing, but it also broke the federal logjam. Shortly after, Congress passed Cap & Trade legislation and the threat of acidification rapidly diminished, at least until now, when the era of Climate Chaos is again raising acidification issues. There is compelling evidence that elevating levels of $CO_2$ in the atmosphere are acidifying oceans. Guess what happens to life on Earth when extra-hot oceans acidify beyond a critical point?

Anyway, at our celebratory gathering after Minnesota enacted its standard and control plan back in '86, the enviros gave me an award for using the words "jeremiad" and "obfuscation" in the same sentence, as my legal brief described the weeping and wailing and gnashing of power company teeth as they failed to create the confusion required to avoid being held accountable for their polluting wastes.

NAWO continued intervening in many electric utility decision-making proceedings including electric rate cases, certificates of need for power plants and powerlines and nuclear waste storage facilities, conservation improvement program (CIP) dockets, and a bunch of legislative battles. NAWO was on the point of the Prairie Island nuclear waste fight with Northern States Power Company (now Xcel Energy), which lasted eight years. The fight started out in 1987 before the Minnesota Environmental Quality Board (MEQB) with a flawed Environmental Impact Statement that remained flawed when the MEQB approved it a year later, then went before the Minnesota Public Utilities Commission where NSP got a flawed Certificate of Need in 1992, so we took it to state courts who agreed with us that the flaws could only be addressed by the Minnesota Legislature, which settled the matter, sort of, after a brutal legislative fight that consumed the entire 1994 legislative session. At the end of it, Jim Howard, CEO of NSP at the time, told me he was finding me a job protecting panthers in the Everglades.

The actual result of the settlement, however, was that the electric utility industry in North America got dragged kicking and screaming into the Modern Era of utility scale renewable energy. In exchange, NSP got dry cask storage of high-level nuclear waste right next to the Prairie Island Mdewakanton Dakota Reservation, another fine example of nuclear racism. Within a few years, however, NSP (by then Xcel Energy) began bragging about how it was leading the nation's power companies in renewable energy development.

NAWO continued participating in various administrative and legislative proceedings throughout the new century's first decade. This included intervening in a powerline Certificate of Need proceeding before the Minnesota Public Utilities Commission (MPUC), to authorize new transmission capacity required to deliver to load centers the new wind generated electricity required by 1994 legislature. NAWO supported the authorization of the new powerlines, with the condition, accepted by the MPUC, that twenty percent of the new wind capacity be owned by members of the communities where the power was generated.

I relate these bits of my involvement with electric utility decision-making as evidence of my understanding regarding how the electric utility industry is managed and regulated, and to provide a foundation for the proposition that properly reforming electric utility management and regulatory structures offer massive benefits to society on a multidimensional basis.

So, what is a properly managed and regulated electric utility industry? It is CLEAR: clean, local, equitable, affordable and reliable. All the technologies required to get from where we are to where we need to be with a CLEAR energy future are readily available and very cost-effective. The problem is that those with vested interests in the existing electric utility industry are only interested in such a transition to the extent that they are able to maintain operational control of electric utility markets, and ownership of the facilities that serve those markets.

To understand the nature of this challenge, a bit of background information is in order.

For starters, this massive industry has US assets in power plants and powerlines that have a value approaching $3,000,000,000,000.00. Three thousand billion dollars. Essentially, all this money is invested into one giant machine that covers the North American continent, divided into three regions. East of the Rocky Mountains, roughly, is the Eastern Interconnection region. West of the Rockies is the Western Interconnection region. Then, there's Texas. All the power plants in each of these regions are connected with high-voltage powerlines, which means that the turbine generating electricity in each power plant is precisely synchronized with the turbines in all the other power plants in the region to maintain the sixty hertz frequency used in North America. Not only must the sixty Hz cycle be maintained, but the amount of power all these interconnected power plants produce must precisely match, in every instant of every day, the varying amounts of electricity energy consumers require throughout the day. (In Europe, the power grid is operated on a fifty hertz frequency.) The connections between regions are weaker, but transmission connections do exist so that in emergencies, power can be transmitted from one region to another. Remember the Texas blackout of 2022? In that time, the connections between Texas and the other regions were not quite strong enough.

This machine is the biggest, and, by far, the most complicated machine humans have ever built. It is the largest capital formation humans have ever amassed. This giant machine produces somewhere around 4,230 billion kilowatt hours of electricity per year, and assuming the average price of electricity is around $0.18/kWh, the revenue stream generated by this machine is in the neighborhood of $760 billion per year. It is the job of about two million people in the United States to keep this machine running, not including lobbyists. There are lots and lots of lobbyists because this giant machine makes lots of money, and it does not want to change. But changes are required, and along with persistent and informed involvement from people in their own communities, it will take legislative action at the state and federal levels to make the necessary changes. Hence the multitude of utility lobbyists working diligently to preserve the status quo.

But the sheer size of the electric utility industry, and the basic foundation that energy services provide for all the multitude of activities it takes to maintain a functioning society, also means that the reformations required by the CLEAR vision for delivering electric utility services will contribute durable solutions to many, and maybe most of the seemingly intractable problems that plague humanity. When we get energy right, we'll be much more able to get the rest of it right, because we'll have the power to do so.

The transition to clean electric utility services will dramatically improve pollution problems in many, many ways. It will eliminate the need to burn coal for all but the most energy-dense industrial loads. Metals production, for example, requires huge amounts of power at very specific locations, and for now, coal provides a solution for that purpose. In those limited sectors where dense power is required, it would be a relatively simple adjustment to require pollution control equipment to scrub the acids and the metals from coal combustion flue gasses, and capture and sequester the carbon. By limiting coal fires to only those functions that require dense energy, pollution abatement strategies become much more manageable and much less expensive.

Completing the energy transition would reduce the need to burn coal in the United States by somewhere around eighty billion tons per year. This reduction alone would be enough to stop global $CO_2$ emissions from increasing, which is the necessary first step to mitigate the impacts of global Climate Chaos. It would also reduce public health problems caused by the release of tens of thousands of tons per year of toxic metals, including mercury, arsenic, beryllium, cadmium, chromium, nickel and selenium, above and beyond reduced incidents of asthma and other respiratory diseases.

The transition to clean electric utility services will also eliminate the need to burn natural gas, which accounts for about thirty-eight percent of US electrical generation, and oil, which contributes about one percent. While both can be burned relatively cleanly, the by-products of pure combustion are carbon dioxide and water. As carbon dioxide is the dominant greenhouse gas, eliminating these sources along with coal would be enough to tip the global scales and actually begin the process of *reducing* the amount of heat-trapping gasses dumped into Earth's atmosphere annually. In addition, oil and gas extraction tend to be concentrated close to each other, and much of the global tension that leads to warring is caused by struggles to control the land where these resources are located. This warring, of course, accelerates Climate Chaos. Blood for gas and oil is not clean.

Many people believe that nuclear power provides an important part of the solution to Climate Chaos. This belief does not withstand informed scrutiny for economic reasons, reasons of public safety and public health, profound social justice and equity issues, and overwhelming environmental concerns. We will examine problems with commercial nuclear power in Chapter 6.

The second element of the CLEAR vision for our energy future is "local." "Local" means within your county, or municipality or within the footprint of the electrical substation(s) that serve a given community. When the electricity consumed by a community is also produced within that community, the money produced by the sale of that electricity to local consumers creates wealth within that local community because instead of getting extracted in service of some distant owner, it gets spent on local goods and services, and circulates within the community many times over. We will explain why this is important as we discuss "equity" and "reliability" aspects below, but for now, suffice it to say that except for the host community, large, central station power plants do not meet this criterion.

The third element is "equitable." This means that *everyone,* regardless of race, religion, country of origin or any other quirk or foible is entitled to clean, affordable and reliable power. Unfortunately, even now, electric utility services get delivered differently for affluent suburban communities than they do for inner city communities with large minority populations. Compare outage rates and durations, and you will find disparities. Many poorer rural communities also suffer from such disparities, and without conscious and deliberate action to correct these inequities, they will only get worse as Climate Chaos ravages above-ground infrastructure, such as the poles and wires that deliver power to peoples' homes.

Further, electric utility services are not being delivered equitably when a wealthy household spends maybe two or five percent of its monthly income on electricity, while a family struggling financially will pay thirty percent or more of its monthly income on electricity. Power plant pollution also raises equity issues because, for example, fish contaminated with mercury has a much more profound impact on people who rely on fish as a dietary protein staple than it does on a tourist eating a shore lunch. As we will discuss further in Chapter 6, the nuclear fuel chain and it is a chain, not a cycle, adds several particularly pernicious aspects to energy equity issues.

Another dimension of the "equitable energy services" concept is connected to the "local" criteria and involves economic democracy. This raises questions regarding costs and benefits assessed and afforded to ratepayers compared to those of shareholders of Investor Owned Utilities (IOUs); about why shareholders of publicly regulated monopoly companies, a significant portion of which are not part of the communities served by the monopoly, are allowed to siphon off the wealth created by providing energy services to that community. What would happen if, instead of this wealth being siphoned off to pay foreign capital interests, it was instead used where it was produced to provide for community interests?

These questions are possible because, during the past twenty years or so, economies of scale have shifted dramatically in the electric utility industry, and we will get to that shortly. But a consequence of this shift is that energy resources are no longer harvested at discrete locations such as mines, and energy production no longer comes from a relatively few very large electric generators. Rather, renewable energy uses lots and lots of individual, distinct components, like solar panels and wind turbines, and they can be located anywhere that it is economically viable to site them.

A major issue, however, perhaps THE major issue, arises because what is economically viable, or, indeed, desirable in terms of siting wind and solar infrastructure from the perspective of serving a particular community is vastly different from the formation of wind and solar technologies that are optimally profitable from the perspective of a private capital formation or of corporate shareholders and the managers of that corporation.

These interests are actually diametrically opposed to each other. Understanding the concept of "capacity factor" is central to understanding this conflict between corporate and community interests. "Capacity factor" refers to the amount of power an electric generator actually produces as a fraction of what it would produce if it were producing all the electricity it could possibly produce over a given period of time, usually measured on an annual basis. For example, if a 1,000-watt generator (which is one kilowatt, or one kW) generated 8,760 kilowatt hours in a year, it would have a capacity factor of 100 percent. It could not physically produce any more than that. In reality, it won't produce that much because sometime during that year, it will be shut off for maintenance, or the wind isn't blowing hard enough for maximum production, or the sun goes behind a cloud, or because it must curtail production because there is not enough demand for electricity at a given time, or a powerline that delivers the electricity to the load got blown over in a storm. The very highest capacity factors for wind turbines, where the turbines are sited in a location that is the windiest, approach fifty percent. A very high capacity factor for solar power is twenty-five percent.

So, if you are a corporate player, your intent is to maximize the amount of power generated by your investment into your wind and solar farms. Your interests are therefore served by cramming as much wind and/or solar generating capacity as possible in those regions that have the highest capacity factors, the richest wind and solar resources: where the wind blows the hardest for the most extended periods of time, and where there are the most hours in a year when sunlight strikes the Earth. Your development model mimics the conventional, historical central station development scenario in which very large generators serve remote loads by transmitting power long distances over high-voltage transmission lines. Your problem, of course, is that now you have tons of electrical generation located far from the consumers who will purchase the electricity you produce. The obvious solution to your problem is to get those consumers to pay for the transmission infrastructure it takes to deliver your power to them. This corporate model dominates renewable energy development in the United States, and ignorant public officials and community leaders are calling for more of it.

If, however, you want what is best economically for your particular community where the wind blows, but not as hard or as often, and where sunshine meets the Earth but not quite as much because you have more clouds or abide in a higher latitude, your best interests are not served by purchasing from remote generators owned by outside interests, while you also pay for the powerlines needed to deliver their electricity to your meter. Rather, your interests are served in two primary ways when wind and solar generation get strategically sized to fit within or close to your community, and get interconnected with neighboring communities and the grid for reliability purposes.

The first, obviously, is that you are not paying for powerlines that outside interests use to extract wealth from your community, and we will discuss an approach to transmission development that is rational in due course. Second, the capital requirement for developing wind and solar capacity to serve a specific community vastly differs from the huge capital formations corporate players access to build their remote wind and solar farms. A community-based approach to renewable energy development amounts up to no more than several tens of millions of dollars per development, as opposed to hundreds of millions of dollars for big remote projects. Therefore, community members have the opportunity to participate in the ownership structure that provides electric utility services to their community. Then, instead of exporting wealth to serve outside corporate interests, the wealth generated by providing those services gets circulated within the community, creating good-paying jobs and expanding opportunities for local economic development.

Finally, a vital aspect of equitable energy has to do with who benefits from developing the renewable energy infrastructure needed to avoid the worst of the intensifying storm, and who experiences adverse consequences of that development. This question is completely overlooked by the more mainstream environmental and safe energy advocates who openly claim to be agnostic as to who owns the required renewable energy infrastructure. "We don't care who owns it," they say, "we just want to get it done." Usually, they then proceed with legislative and/or regulatory campaigns that set renewable energy standards with which power companies must comply. This approach guarantees failure, as evidenced by the fact the storm continues to intensify even though many state standards for renewable energy have been in place for almost twenty years, and that the development model is almost exclusively concentrated on remote electrical generation development with expensive, publicly financed transmission infrastructure.

To get enough renewable energy online soon enough to make a difference, however, an awful lot needs to happen very quickly. Yet, repeatedly in the news we hear stories about people from communities that are affected by wind or solar projects complaining about adverse impacts that development has on their lives. Perhaps they find the development unsightly, or the flicker of turbine blades annoying. Perhaps the development interferes with their ability to continue the farming practices that have been in place for generations. Maybe the construction of a large wind or solar farm requires significant investment into local roads and bridges, and allocation of the costs for the upgrades falls unfairly, or is perceived to fall unfairly, on the local population while the developers get another free lunch. All these sorts of issues, whatever they may be, retard the development of the technologies humanity so desperately needs, perhaps fatally.

In this light, it is helpful to remember that large, positive, transformational changes in society tend to happen more quickly and with less disruption when members of that society are motivated to make the change, as opposed to when they are ordered to do so. Or, as one of the powerline protesters told me over forty years ago, "Pig shit stinks," he said, "but if they're your pigs, it smells like money."

Affordability is the next element of CLEAR to be considered, which of course is closely linked to what is equitable. Low-income households pay a higher percentage, sometimes a much higher percentage of their monthly income for energy services than do higher income households. While most jurisdictions have some provision to prevent utility shut-offs when outside temperatures are extremely cold or extremely hot, this is but a basic first step on a long path toward equity. Energy services, like health care and other basic needs, are or ought to be human rights that are built into our social structures. The unfortunate reality is that in the United States today, fundamental human rights take a hit when they bump up against shareholder earnings. That's why we need a stronger movement.

Reliability factors round out the CLEAR vision of our energy future. While it is certainly true that most existing electric utility systems perform reasonably well in terms of power outages, especially for the more affluent neighborhoods in their service territories, reliability continues to be a major issue for Communities of Color and poorer communities. In all instances, however, as storms and other extreme events intensify, reliability requirements will demand that more of the power distribution infrastructure gets put underground. Without a dramatic change in the application of social justice, Communities of Color and poorer communities will be the last to be afforded this protection.

But there is a darker side to reliability issues that is brought on by a political reality that includes sabotage and terrorist activity. In 1982

Hunter and Amory Lovins wrote a book about it entitled *Brittle Power* that was commissioned by the Pentagon and re-released after 9/11. The book first came out on the heels of our powerline fight across North Dakota and West Central Minnesota, during which powerline protesters repeatedly downed power towers, shot out insulators, arced out conductors and so forth, so at least superficially, it was fairly easy for Amory and Hunter to document how an electrical power system dominated by central station technology is vulnerable to disruption, both accidental and by design. The book's analysis has been borne out on several occasions recently as news outlets carried stories of disgruntled extremist citizens attacking substations.

Remember, the electrical power system in North America is all one big machine, all hooked together by the high-voltage transmission grid. Grid intersections are substations. This system has been developed and enhanced over the past century or so, and is designed to manage an electrical system in which electrical generation is dominated by a relatively few very large central station power plants. The interconnectedness of this system provides some increased reliability in managing weather-related events, because when a storm comes through and knocks out some critical component, the interconnectedness allows neighboring regions to fill the gap. However, the primary benefit of interconnectedness since electric utility markets got deregulated in the 1990s, is that it enables the economic dispatch of power generators, which we will examine shortly.

A consequence of that interconnectedness is that it makes the system brittle. Reliability factors are in play because a small and well-trained team of sappers could simultaneously take out just a tiny handful of strategically located substations, which would blackout virtually the entire continent east of the Mississippi River. To borrow Amory and Hunter's analogy, this vulnerability is why trees do not have just three or four very large leaves. One of the major improvements enabled by the transition away from central station power and into a renewable energy future is that an extremely large number of generators dispersed and distributed across the land dramatically improves the resiliency of the system from a security perspective.

(The term "dispersed generation" refers to electricity generators of no particular size but generally much smaller than central station power plants. They are located in geographically diverse locations and connected to the existing transmission and distribution system. Dispersed generation is not tied to a specific load, and all the power dispersed generators produce flows into the grid. "Distributed generation" tends to refer to small-scale power projects, defined in Minnesota law as ten MW or less, built to meet on-site power requirements at a particular location, with net excess power flowing into the grid via an interconnection. In some instances, the terms are used interchangeably.)

More civilized reliability factors, as opposed to terrorist activities, come into play as utility systems transition from reliance upon conventional fuel sources, which are more or less dispatchable on demand and can essentially be turned "off" and "on" with a switch, to intermittent renewable energy resources, depending on whether the sun is shining or the wind is blowing in specific locations. Part of the answer to this issue has to do with how renewable technologies get deployed, because while the wind isn't always blowing at a specific spot, it is always blowing somewhere. Similarly with the relationship between solar power and clouds during daytime hours. So, as more renewable energy generation gets deployed in a dispersed and distributed manner throughout a region, the higher will be the capacity factor for that deployment.

As society becomes more reliant on renewable energy resources, energy storage systems become the key to being able to dispatch power on demand. Battery technologies have made huge strides in the past decade and will likely make further advancements between the time of this writing and your reading of it. And this leads back to the "clean" part of CLEAR, in that to the extent that Lithium and other minerals need to be extracted from the Earth to enable the dispatchability of modern electric utility systems, that extraction must absolutely minimize the disruption and contamination of surrounding ecosystems.

Unless human society is able to *quickly* correct market and regulatory flaws that reward destructive energy management practices by electric utilities, the ecological foundation our regulatory systems require to function will continue to disintegrate at an accelerating pace. The evidence is everywhere. How did it come to be that the energy institutions responsible for removing much of the drudgery from human existence, and that provide for so many of our creature comforts and basic needs, are also driving human civilization, such as it is, toward an apocalyptic end? Yet, it is also true that a relatively few common sense corrections to those flaws promise an abundance of prosperity.

# Chapter 3
## A Few Basics and A Bit of History

The electric utility system is endlessly complicated, and the planning and engineering required to make it work includes the application of imaginary numbers as sine waves on the sixty Hertz cycle of the alternating current transmission grid must be managed to remain synchronized. So some basic information is required in order to understand what is going on, and to be taken seriously by politicians and utility managers and regulators when individuals and people in their own communities get organized enough to propose corrections to the flaws that will prove fatal unless they are corrected. For instance, what is the difference between a kilowatt and a megawatt hour? Those who are functionally illiterate about energy are unlikely to contribute much to decision-making proceedings, although it is also true that in certain settings, as they say, the power of ignorant people in large numbers should not be underestimated.

A kilowatt is a measure of electrical capacity equal to 1,000 watts. If you were to take ten 100-watt lightbulbs, and turn them all on at the same time, it would require one kilowatt (1 kW = 100 watts per bulb X 10 lightbulbs) of generation capacity to light them all up simultaneously. If you want to keep all ten of those hundred-watt lightbulbs burning for one hour, you will need one kilowatt-*hour* (kWh) of electrical energy to do so. Electrical energy, or kWhs, are what shows up on your electric bill. Electrical capacity is measured in watts, and electrical energy is measured in watt/hours. 1,000 watts equals a kilowatt; 1,000 kilowatts equal a megawatt (MW); 1,000 MW equals a gigawatt (GW) in terms of capacity, and similarly for watt hours, kWhs and MWhs of energy. A typical central station power plant has an electrical generating capacity of many hundreds of MW, some more than a thousand. In contrast, a typical solar panel has an electrical generating capacity of 250 – 400 watts, which is why solar generation projects are versatile, and can be designed to be whatever size you want. A typical utility-scale wind turbine is in the range of two to ten MW, with the larger ones being offshore.

Capacity factors (CFs) also need to be understood. CFs measure how much energy a unit of generation would produce if it were generating 100 percent of its rated capacity all 8,760 hours in a year, which nothing does. Repairs, maintenance, refueling for nuclear reactors, cloudy days and the dark of night for solar panels, reduced wind speeds for wind turbines, and increasingly, drought conditions in our changing climate all cut in to capacity factors. If a wind turbine with a rated capacity of two MW generated 7,008,000 kWh in a year, it would have a capacity factor of forty for that year, which is pretty good for a wind turbine. (2MW = 2,000 kW x 8,760 hr./yr. = 17,520,000 kWh/yr. x 0.4 (CF) = 7,008,000 kWh/yr.) And remember, watts = amps x volts, where watts are units of power, amps are the magnitude of the power current, and volts describe the force of the current flow.

With that foundational information, let's look briefly at a bit of history regarding how the electric utility industry evolved.

Thomas Edison organized the world's first electric utility in New York in 1880, a couple years after he turned an incandescent light bulb into a commercial product. While Edison gets most of the credit in popular parlance for ushering in the era of electricity, we should recognize that much of the inventing in that time was actually done by Nikola Tesla, who introduced the world to alternating current, dynamos, transformers, motors, induction coils, and check him out to see what else. In any event, from the 1880s through the 1930s and well into the 1950s, private companies and municipalities all across the country invested in their own relatively small boiler, mostly coal-fired, maybe a few fired by gas or oil. Then they strung up wires throughout their communities, and before too long, most everyone living within city limits had access to electric utility services. It was a big deal when a municipality got big enough and wealthy enough to afford to have a power company. But the wires stopped at the edge of town because it was one thing to hook up meters when there were ten or twenty or more houses per square block, but it was way too expensive to string wires in the country when there would be at most, maybe a few electric meters per mile.

Therefore, throughout most of that period of time, people living in the country or in smaller rural communities continued to rely on kerosene lamps if they wanted to read a book or milk the cows after dark. In 1935, President Roosevelt signed Executive Order 7073 and the Rural Electrification Administration (REA) was created to establish power cooperatives that would bring power to the countryside, which happened slowly and wasn't more or less complete until some decades later.

As increasing numbers of people, mostly in cities but slowly spreading out, began enjoying electric utility services, and as more gadgets and gizmos were devised to be powered by electricity, the demand for power grew. So the private company or municipal power authority serving a community had to either build a bigger power plant or get another generating unit to keep up with the demand. Engineers being how they are, it did not take them long to figure out that as they built generators bigger, each kW of generation capacity got cheaper. While the *price* of a twenty MW generator is much more than the price of a five MW generator, the cost to construct and operate each installed kW in a twenty MW generator was substantially cheaper than the cost to build and operate each installed kW of a five MW generator. So they biggered them. And they biggered them. And then they biggered them some more. This trend continued for decades until power plants got so big that several of them exploded because things like co-efficiencies of expansion got out of control, or the cost of shutting down a whole power plant just because some relatively small component failed became prohibitive.

These economies of scale produced the Central Station Era of electrical generation. Society is still in the tail end of that, and how quickly we get out of it will be a significant factor in determining the extent of havoc wreaked by Climate Chaos. In the Central Station Era, each humongous power plant, whether it gets fueled by gas or coal or uranium, (oil peaking plants are usually a lot smaller) was built to accommodate site-specific characteristics at its location. Coal plants were designed to optimize the combustion of coal from specific mines. Large components, like boilers, were explicitly designed for each specific plant, manufactured individually, shipped to the site and incorporated into the machine. Each central station power plant got custom built.

What the biggering did, of course, was make all the smaller, older generators owned and operated by private companies and municipalities less competitive in energy markets because when electricity from a bigger power plant became available, it reduced the price that consumers had to pay per kWh of consumption. As a result, the electric utility industry began to consolidate. By the 1940s, through the 1950s and into the '60s, as older generators wore out and needed to be replaced, and as municipal officials saw the greener grass on the other side of the fence, so to speak, Investor Owned Utilities (IOUs) tended to buy out smaller companies and municipal power authorities because their big new machines could produce electricity cheaper and more reliably than their competition. The smaller IOU companies disappeared, as did most municipals. IOUs became by far the dominant players in the industry, and by 2022, they served about seventy-two percent of the US electric utility market. The remaining customers are served primarily by REA coops and surviving municipal power agencies.

As a federal agency, the REA could not get bought out by expanding IOUs. And being as its market was so dispersed, thereby making it too expensive for bottom-line capitalists to bother with, it was not much affected directly by the industry's consolidation. Also, while the REA operates coal plants, another primary source of REA power was dams in the Tennessee Valley, and along the Missouri and Colorado Rivers and other river systems managed by the US Army Corps of Engineers. IOUs therefore had limited access to hydropower in the United States. The REA business model created Generation & Transmission (G&T) Cooperatives which are responsible for generating and transmitting power to their member local distribution cooperatives, which served rural consumers.

Across the country, something a bit over 450 municipal power agencies also survived the consolidation, including, in Minnesota, the Rochester Public Utilities and other members of the Southern Minnesota Municipal Power Agency. Municipal power agencies that survived were able to do so primarily because their leadership was wise enough to understand the larger value of a community-based electric utility to the community it served and was therefore able to look beyond the cheaper power put on the table by the IOUs. While these municipals retained their own community identity, they often purchased the electricity used by their customers after negotiating a deal with a locally dominant IOU. In other instances, they became junior partners in big central station power plants owned predominantly by an IOU.

Unfortunately, both the REA electric coops and the surviving municipals were routinely treated like weak and perhaps intellectually challenged younger siblings by the IOUs and other players in the utility industry, like coal companies.

My first experience with the dynamics of these condescending relationships occurred when I got involved with the fight over the 800 kV direct current (DC) powerline across North Dakota and West Central Minnesota. By the 1970s, the local distribution REA coops serving most of rural Minnesota were going strong and had organized themselves into two G&T power coops, United Power Association and Cooperative Power Association. (These two G&Ts have since consolidated themselves to form Great River Energy.) Much of the power consumed by UPA/CPA distribution coop members at the time was generated by dams along the Missouri River that were built and operated by the US Army Corps of Engineers, and managed by the Western Area Power Administration, which operates within the US Department of Energy and only serves cooperative and municipal power agencies, and most of the rest was purchased by UPA/CPA from Upper Midwest IOUs.

But there's a limit to how much power WAPA can produce, so as UPA/CPA grew, they decided it was time to build their own power plant just west of the Missouri River near Underwood, North Dakota and transmit the electricity into Minnesota via the DC powerline. They called it the CU Project, which included a 1,200 MW power plant called Coal Creek Station and the DC powerline, and they did a poor enough job of it in every aspect to cause an organized revolt by UPA/CPA coop member-consumers beginning in the mid-1970s and continuing well into the 1980s. The conflict was intense enough to cause the late Senator Paul Wellstone and his colleague, Dr. Barry M. Casper, to get involved with the fight and to write an absolutely fascinating and instructive book about it entitled, *POWERLINE: The First Battle of America's Energy War*. It was this conflict that caused me in 1977 to begin my career of attempting to guide electric utility management toward decisions that better reflect public interests, and I have many stories about my adventures during that time.

For present purposes, however, the Coal Creek Station is a mine-mouth power plant immediately adjacent to the Falkirk Mine which supplies all the lignite coal that fuels Coal Creek Station. The mine is wholly owned by North American Coal Corporation. In the mid-1970s, as the project was getting underway, UPA/CPA officials negotiated a contract with North American Coal Corporation that required North American Coal to deliver all the lignite Coal Creek Station would need for $0.18 per million Btu of thermal energy. UPA/CPA managers all congratulated themselves on their good deal, as the going rate at the time was closer to $0.30 per million Btu. But the ink was still not dry on the contract when North American Coal Corporation unilaterally jacked the price of lignite for Coal Creek Station by more than 5-fold, to $1.00 per million Btu. Then the bumpkins managing UPA/CPA all got glum as they acquiesced without protest to North American Coal's thievery and took their frustrations out on their own coop members with management practices that included telling them that, "We're going to shove this powerline down your throat, and we're going to make you like it." They continued to let their coop members get ripped off for the next 40+ years until 2022, when they sold Coal Creek Station in the deregulated wholesale power market to an outfit called Rainbow Energy Center.

I got to experience another example of how dominant players in the industry used smaller players to their own advantage when NSP, in the early 1980s, decided it would build two new 600 MW coal-fired power plants, Sherco 3 & 4, near Becker, Minnesota, on the Mississippi River right next to Sherco Units 1 & 2, which had come online in the mid-1970s. However, before proceedings to certify and license the new units even began, NSP realized that it's energy and demand forecasts were so far off that it unilaterally dropped plans for Sherco 4. Then NSP realized that its internal load requirements would not even support Unit 3, so to justify building Sherco 3, it roped two relatively small municipal associations, the Southern Minnesota Municipal Power Agency and United Minnesota Municipal Power Agency, into becoming junior Sherco 3 partners. NSP needed SMMPA and UMMPA to own forty-one percent of Sherco 3.

Lea and I, along with Wendel, a physics professor from Gustavus Adolphus College in St. Peter, Minnesota, teamed up to intervene in the Certificate of Need proceeding for Sherco 3 in 1981. We formed an organization we called TKO, "The Kilowatt Organization," and our logo showed Ready Kilowatt giving raspberries on a letterhead that read, "You Megawatt, We Kilowatt." During the proceeding, which lasted from early February 1982 well into the summer, I got to watch the lawyers representing UMMPA and SMMPA sit placidly and mute, day after day, as NSP lawyers used UMMPA and SMMPA energy and demand requirements to make up the difference NSP needed to justify in the minds of regulators the certification of Sherco 3. Then, energy consumers in UMMPA and SMMPA municipalities got to also participate in the rate increases needed to pay for Sherco 3, and some were not pleased. UMMPA merged into SMMPA in 1984.

Anyway, with economies of scale driving the industry toward ever bigger and more expensive power plants that produced ever bigger amounts of increasingly cheaper power, IOUs quickly became natural monopolies. In an industry driven by these economies, relatively small pools of capital, each in its own community and managing a relatively expensive product, did not stand a chance.

Being monopolies have the nature that they have, the need for regulation soon became apparent. Therefore, early in the twentieth century, Public Utilities Commissions, which historically had been primarily focused on railroads, became involved with regulating gas and electric utilities. In Wisconsin, Georgia, and elsewhere, they're called Public *Service* Commissions. Either way, their job then and to this day includes regulating the price of delivering electric utility *services*. There are a thousand historical accounts of how these commissions around the country behaved and misbehaved, some being more salacious than others. For our purposes, however, one would think the name and the function of these regulatory bodies would be a clue. But no. The overwhelming failure of electric utility regulators to actually serve public interests is caused by the fundamental contradiction we have previously noted: they regulate the price of a commodity when they should be regulating the cost of getting public services delivered.

If regulators weren't failing, the companies they regulate in the public interest would not be a major, if not *the* driving force accelerating Climate Chaos. Energy services would be universal and affordable for everyone, and wealth would not get stripped away from communities as part of the price of the power they consume. In my mind, anyway, not polluting the atmosphere, and affordable, universal energy services that enhance the economic well-being of the community being served, are all vital parts of serving public interests.

Of course, the companies they regulate are not failing financially because it's *really* hard to fail financially when your regulated business is guaranteed a financial profit by its regulators.

The way it works, essentially, is that the power company tells the regulator how much electricity it expects to sell in its "test" year, based on energy forecasts. Then utility lawyers and regulatory bureaucrats argue about the correct number until they reach an agreement. Once energy requirements get established, the power company tells the regulator how much money it needs to spend in order to produce all the electricity it has forecast and expects to sell during the "test" year. That amount of money includes all the payments required to pay for the power plants used to serve its load, and all the powerlines and substations it needs to deliver power to consumers, and all the equipment it takes to make it all work, all appropriately amortized and depreciated. All of that is called the rate-base, and utility lawyers and regulatory bureaucrats argue until they come to an agreement as to what precisely is the correct and proper amount of money in the rate-base for the test year.

Once the rate-base gets established, the bureaucrats and utility lawyers argue over what precisely should be the rate-of-return on that rate-base. Usually, it's somewhere in the range of nine to eleven percent, and that profit margin gets baked into the rates paid by consumers.

After that, utility lawyers and regulatory bureaucrats reach an agreement regarding all the expenses attached to managing the rate-base, including all the salaries and benefits of all its employees, and all the bonuses for its corporate officers, and all the advertisements it needs to tell its customers how good it is. Then those expenses are added to the pile of money already established as the rate-base and its proper rate-of-return. Finally, utility lawyers and regulatory bureaucrats come to a conclusion about the cost of all the fuel it will take to produce the power in the test year forecast, and they add that to the pile. Fuel costs are volatile, however, and that is why you see a "fuel adjustment clause" on your electric bill, which causes the price you pay per kWh to fluctuate between rate cases depending on the amount of money the power company actually needs to spend for fuel during any particular billing period.

Once the Public Utilities/Service Commission settles all those costs and expenses and determines the proper rate-of-return, the total revenue requirement of the utility for the "test year" is established. Then it becomes a matter of allocating appropriate portions of that total revenue requirement among the various classes of residential, commercial, and industrial consumers, and to various categories of consumers within those classes, such as those who participate in a peak curtailment program, or time-of-day rates, being as it is more expensive to generate electricity when everybody is consuming it, as opposed to when most people are asleep, or, these days, participating in a solar program, and so forth. Then it all gets boiled down to the cents per kilowatt-hour, and taxes and fees and adjustments that appear on your electric bill.

Two additional types of forecasting energy and capacity requirements are also vital components of electric utility management. Short-term and day-ahead forecasts inform the dispatch order that determines which specific power plants will serve energy markets at every given point in time as energy consumption ebbs and flows according to load duration curves. Load duration curves follow a very similar pattern, day by day, throughout the year. As most people get started in the morning, energy requirements increase as they eat breakfast and get ready for the day. Energy requirements continue increasing as industry and commerce get to work, and tend to reach their maximum in mid-to-late weekday afternoon, and then taper off as people return home and settle in for the evening. The daily load duration curve then drops off later at night when most of us go to sleep. These curves follow seasonal patterns, and they have spikes during hotter summer afternoons due to elevated air conditioning loads, and during colder winter days due to heating requirements.

Throughout most of the Central Station Era, the dispatch order of electric generators has been relatively straight forward. The monopoly-owned power plants that produce the "cheapest" electricity come online first and stay online 24/7 until they need to shut down for maintenance or repair, or in the case of nuclear reactors, for refueling. These are the Central Station Era "baseload" plants that serve the load regardless of what electrical requirements are at any point in the load duration curve. Next in the dispatch order are "intermediate" plants that have the ability to ramp up electrical generation in the morning as things get started, and to ramp down in the evening when things slow down. Intermediate plants tend to be coal or gas fired. Peaking plants are the most expensive to operate because they are mostly oil and sometimes gas fired, but this enables them to start up and shut down quickly, and they only come online during periods of peak demand or in emergencies.

These are Central Station Era definitions.

Since around the turn of the 21st century, however, whole new dimensions to load duration curves have become important. In 1996, the Federal Energy Regulatory Commission (FERC) issued orders that deregulated wholesale electric markets and set the conditions for competition in those markets. (Remember ENRON? ENRON was one of the first independent power producers to enter the deregulated market. ENRON cheated and got busted, and then one of the world's biggest companies disappeared.) Up until the 1996 FERC orders, each power company was responsible for serving the load within its service territory, which was and remains defined by regulation. These service territories were linked together with high-voltage powerlines primarily for security purposes, so that in emergencies, power could be transmitted to neighboring service territories that were experiencing emergency situations.

The deregulation of wholesale energy markets dramatically changed the function of the interconnected high-voltage transmission system, which in turn raises fundamental equity issues over who bene-fits from the way in which the system is used, and who pays the cost of making that infrastructure available. Instead of primarily performing a reliability function, the high-voltage system became the "highway" for bulk power transfers that serve the economic interests of large in-stitutional players in electric utility markets. Deregulation made it pos-sible for Independent Power Producers (IPPs) to compete with IOUs for market share. While some consumers see some financial benefit on their energy bills due to the economic dispatch made possible by deregulating wholesale markets, all consumers in most regulated con-sumer markets see significant increases on their energy bills to pay the many tens of billions of dollars needed across the country to construct all the additional high-voltage transmission that deregulated economic dispatch of generation requires.

After the deregulation of wholesale energy markets, any enti-ty with Qualifying Facilities (QFs, which were established in 1978 under the Public Utility Regulatory Policies Act, or PURPA) was able to enter the competition to serve specific, designated wholesale markets by putting in its bid to the Independent System Operator (ISO) that served its region of the continent. The continent was divided up into about ten designated regions, and you can search online for ISO to see where they are. The FERC orders created the ISOs, and each ISO manages the competition within its designated region by dispatching power to match the load duration curve ac-cording to the price bid by each market participant. Each market participant tells the ISO how much power it has to sell, and the lowest price it is willing to accept for that power. There are long-term bids, and day-ahead bids, and various other categories, and as the load duration curve rises in the morning, the ISO dispatches generation to match the increasing load, with the next "cheapest" bid filling the next increment of needed power. Then, later in the day, the ISO manages power generation reductions by shutting off the most expensive bid power first, and then the next most expensive, and so forth. If you want to know how all that works, check out PURPA and FERC and Independent System Operator online, and follow your nose, so to speak.

Remember, however, that "cheapest power" is a relative term. Anything is cheap if you do not pay for it, and the price energy consumers pay for the electricity they consume does not even begin to pay for the damage caused by utility industry pollution.

A third important category of forecasting comes into play as a tool used by the industry and its regulators to make decisions about how to meet long-term energy and capacity requirements into the future. The conventional way of using this tool is terribly misguided, and we'll get into why that is in due course.

For now, rate structures that determine how electrical energy consumers pay for electric utility services are totally a product of the Central Station Era, in which each unit of production got cheaper as central station power plants got bigger. As that era matured, refinements were made to this basic regulatory framework. For example, for decades, most industrial customers along with bigger commercial customers and a few from the residential sector took advantage of "declining block rate" features in the rate design. This regulatory device divided the monthly energy consumption of a customer into chunks of power. The first chunk was the most expensive, and as more power was consumed during the billing period, the second chunk was cheaper than the first, and the third was cheaper than the second. In essence, this was a very successful "profit sharing" strategy on the part of power companies and their regulators that encouraged customers to use ever increasing amounts of electricity. The Arab Oil Embargo, a growing awareness of the environmental damage cause by utility industry pollution, and the upper limit on economies of scale for central station generators mostly put an end to this practice.

How the electric utility industry and its regulators treated energy conservation provides another example of how rate design matured as the Central Station Era progressed. Initially, and for decades to follow, energy conservation was a foreign concept. There were no conservation programs. To illustrate the point, when I was a kid growing up in Minnesota, the dominant IOU was Northern States Power Company, which had consolidated power production throughout the greater Twin Cities region and beyond into Wisconsin and the Dakotas by buying out scores of little power companies and municipal power authorities. Even though it was a monopoly with no competition, NSP ran ads on the radio and print media, probably on TV too, but I do not know because we did not have one. The ads had Reddy Kilowatt, a red lightning-bolt-like humanoid figure with a lightbulb head, singing a jingle that went, "Electricity is penny cheap, it's penny cheap from NSP to you!"

The Arab Oil Embargo of 1973 changed all that, and energy conservation became a thing of which everybody started to become aware. Conservation suddenly had a place in state energy policies throughout the country, and the value of conservation measures even increased a bit more after the North American Water Office demonstrated their ability to be part of a pollution control strategy during Minnesota's Acid Deposition Control Act proceedings. Energy conservation programs became part of the electric utility regulatory structure, and there was nothing utility managers and shareholders could do to prevent that from happening. CIP, they are usually called, for Conservation Improvement Program. Nevertheless, energy conservation continues to erode electric utility earnings, and so it was considered, from a power company management perspective, as a necessary evil. Orders from electric utility regulators to create and manage energy conservation programs were complied with, but grudgingly, and the results from electric utility conservation programs were, and continue to be puny, paltry things.

Even utility regulators looked at energy conservation as a punishment. To illustrate this point, one of the conditions for allowing NSP (now Xcel Energy) to store high-level nuclear waste in dry storage casks on Prairie Island, was that instead of being ordered to operate conservation programs that spent one and a half percent of electrical energy sales revenue on an annual basis like every other regulated power company in Minnesota, NSP was required to spend two percent on energy conservation as part of the price it had to pay in order to get the nuclear waste dump. Either way, it's a pitiful result, and we'll examine that shortly. For now, the point is that power companies make money by selling electricity, and energy conservation erodes power company earnings, but power companies will be punished in their next rate case if they do not comply with puny and paltry energy conservation requirements. So, in terms of the effectiveness of electric utility conservations programs, maybe ponder a question about how well you actually do things that you are ordered to do, but that, for your own very good reasons, you really do not want to do.

In the late 1980s, before I got in the fight with NSP over nuclear waste storage on Prairie Island that ended all collaboration, I was able to convince NSP management that they could turn energy conservation from a money loser into a profit center with a little regulatory rate reform. While the reform did not solve the contradiction between power company interests in making more money by selling more electricity and societal interests in using energy efficiently, it did enable NSP to think positively about energy conservation to the point where, to this day, Xcel Energy brags about how it has the best energy conservation program in the country. What I told them to do, and what they did, was to get regulatory approval for a performance-based rate design that separated the conservation portion of its rate-base from its supply-side rate-base. Then, as NSP could demonstrate to the satisfaction of its regulators that its investments into conservation did a better job of saving electricity, the rate-of-return on that conservation portion of the rate-base would increase, according to how much energy it could demonstrate that its conservation programs saved. Unfortunately, before we could proceed further in our collaborative efforts, we got involved with the nuclear waste fight and our ability to cooperate with each other totally evaporated.

We will examine in detail how to align power company interests in making money with societal interests in using energy efficiently in due course, and shortly, we will look at how the electric utility paradigm is shifting away from the Central Station Era.

But first, as we have noted, economies of scale in the Central Station Era favored making power plants bigger, and as they got bigger, each unit of production got cheaper. But everything has its limits, of course, and the limit to this expansion in the size of central station power plants was reached when the cost of reinforcing power plant components so they would not explode exceeded the value of the electricity that the larger size would enable to be generated, and when the cost of down-time to repair broken components exceeded the value of the electricity produced by the larger size. Up until those points were reached, the more capacity that was installed in a power plant, the cheaper each unit of capacity became, and the price of power to consumers got reduced accordingly. The Central Station Era would continue so long as the price consumers paid for electricity from central station machines was less than the price consumers would pay for electricity from other sources, such as wind and solar power. By the mid-1990s, it was becoming apparent even to the most fervent supporters of central station power that the renewable energy alternatives were becoming increasingly competitive.

While the cost of wind power was rapidly dropping through the 1980s and into the 1990s, it was still too expensive for utility-scale applications, and up until that time, the public perception was mostly that utility-scale wind does not work. This perception was created in significant part because, during the Carter administration, numerous wind turbine companies in California installed about 16,000 wind turbines, the largest of which was about 350 kW, primarily in the Altamont Pass. The problem was that wind developers were compensated according to how many kW of capacity they installed, rather than how many kilowatt hours of electricity that capacity produced. With nascent technology, scant maintenance budgets and improper incentives, a lot of generation capacity got installed, not much electricity got produced, and the utility industry back then could righteously proclaim that wind do not work.

This was the mindset of NSP and the utility industry in 1994, when a primary result of the Prairie Island nuclear waste fight was that NSP got ordered by law to bring utility-scale wind power to market, but with an off-ramp because there were two increments. The first increment was for 425 MW of wind that NSP could either develop by itself and own the wind turbines, or it could contract for the installation of the wind turbines and purchase the power from the developer and deliver the wind generated electricity to its consumers. If that first increment of 425 megawatts proved to be cost-effective as defined by the Minnesota Public Utilities Commission after a couple years, NSP would then be ordered by law to either develop, or contract for development an additional 400 MW of wind power which NSP would purchase from the developer and deliver it to its customers.

NSP opted to purchase the power instead of owning the turbines and put out a Request for Proposals (RFP) to wind developers for the first increment of 425 MW. When responses were returned, NSP did not like the winning bid because Dan, the developer who submitted it had also testified on behalf of our Prairie Island Coalition seeking to stop the nuclear waste dump on Prairie Island. He testified that nobody would starve while they froze in the dark if NSP did not get its nuclear waste dump. Other options were available, he testified. In retaliation, NSP broke the confidentiality of the bidding process and told another developer, Zond, which later got bought out by ENRON, the numbers it would have to beat to get the bid. Zond beat the numbers and got the bid.

The largest wind turbines Zond was manufacturing at the time, in 1995, were 500 kW machines. But in its bid, Zond told NSP that for its contract with NSP, it would manufacture and deploy 750 kW machines, and that is what it did. Or, perhaps, in order to prove that wind does not work, it was NSP that told Zond to ramp up the size of the turbines by fifty percent all at once without testing. The problem, of course, is that the 750 kW machines are half again as large as 500 kW machines, which means that they have significantly different and more intense stresses on several major components than the smaller turbines. During normal development, when ramping up a technology with so many moving parts that much, multiple components would get tested to failure until it was determined that everything was in fact engineered to be durable enough to withstand the additional stresses created by the larger machines. Zond did none of that. Zond simply increased the size of everything by half, and deployed 300 turbines, each with a capacity of 750 kW. Then, whatever else we did the next couple years, we all waited to see if those turbines would prove to be cost-effective.

NSP was betting that various components of the Zond 750s, particularly the gearboxes which experience enormous stresses as the power of the wind gets converted to electricity, would quickly fail, and that would be the end of that. NSP almost won its bet. Within weeks of the decision by the Minnesota Public Utilities Commission that wind generated electricity was in fact cost-effective, the gear boxes did begin to fail. Within the following year, every one of them had to be replaced. But by then, the order to continue had already been issued, and there was no turning back. For the first time, at least in North America, utility-scale renewable energy had been deployed, and it found its place in the routine dispatch order that determines which electric generation units come online as the load duration curve fluctuates throughout the day. Three years later, after contracting for and receiving power from the required next increment of 400 MW of wind, NSP, then Xcel Energy, was bragging about how it was the nation's leading renewable energy power company. The Central Station Era began to fade, renewable energy achieved deployment at the utility scale, and economies of scale began to shift dramatically.

In short, within the same brief period of time during the 1990s, the electric utility industry underwent two transformative, paradigm-shifting changes: competition entered wholesale markets, and utility-scale renewable energy began to be deployed. Modern Era renewable energy technologies, and the management programs required to deploy them and integrate them into the electric utility system became mature enough in terms of performance, and cheap enough in terms of cost-effectiveness, to gain increasing shares of electric utility markets. In turn, these two factors are in the process of fundamentally changing economies of scale for the industry, which is redefining who gets to participate in the electric utility market, and *that is* a big deal if we make it that far.

The paradigm shift from the Central Station Era to the Modern Era of delivering electric utility services began in earnest in 1994 with the Prairie Island mandates. In the Modern Era, economies of scale will increasingly cause electricity to become cheaper, not as electric generators get bigger, but as more electric generators get manufactured. Instead of each massive generator getting custom built on-site, the components of modern energy technologies all get mass-produced on assembly lines or in batches. While large, utility-scale wind turbines have their various components assembled on-site, all the components, from turbine blades to gearboxes and tower segments, are mass-produced in factories. Solar panels get manufactured and assembled in factories, and fully functional individual panels get delivered for deployment. The Modern Era of delivering electric utility services uses mass-produced components, and the more components of the Modern Era that get manufactured in factories, the cheaper become deployments of wind and solar and all the rest of it.

This shift has profound implications for energy monopolies. As noted earlier, while energy competition has entered *wholesale* energy markets which vastly broadens opportunities for non-regulated utility players to participate in the production of electricity, regulated utilities still, by and large, monopolize retail energy markets where consumers live. You do not get to pick from whom you will purchase your electricity, by and large. This is a remnant of the Central Station Era that now, primarily and increasingly, serves the interests of regulated utility managers and shareholders who own and operate the remaining central station machines, and bureaucrats who resist regulatory reformations needed to optimize the societal benefits of the Modern Era. While there are exceptions in that some jurisdictions allow consumers to purchase their power from an Independent Power Producer, the utility that owns the distribution grid that serves an Independent Power Producer's customer still charges for the service of delivering the independently produced power. But most customers have no choice, and who your power supplier is depends on where you live.

This dramatic shift in economies of scale means that rules and regulations *are the only things* preventing broader participation in the systems that deliver electric utility services. Massive capital formations of hundreds of millions or billions of dollars are no longer a prerequisite for participating in electric utility markets. Whereas, from the dawn of the Central Station Era until it collapses, economies of scale drive the electric utility industry toward larger and larger individual capital formations in service of large and increasing numbers of consumers over a broad service territory, economies of scale in the Modern Era are driving consumers in their own communities toward discrete, strategically sized capital formations in service of their own communities.

Interestingly, shortly after it became evident in the 1980s to electric utility managers that the "buy bigger plants" strategy would no longer work as a business model due to economy-of-scale constraints, within a few years, instead of bigger plants, the business model required a bigger service territory. They all went wild with mergers so they could get big enough to avoid getting eaten by wholesale competitors like ENRON, with endless possibilities. NSP first looked east for its merger partner and was all set to hook up with Wisconsin Electric when scandalous *ex parte* communications between the power company and the Public Service Commission of Wisconsin derailed the deal. A senior NSP Vice President told me they were going to name the merged entity "Primergy" because the good names had all been taken. With Primergy scuttled, NSP looked west to New Century Energies out of Colorado for a partner and the deal to form Xcel Energy got approved by the US Securities & Exchange Commission on August 17, 2000.

As evidenced by the wave of mergers, economies of scale in the Central Station Era require continual growth and expansion of the systems that Central Station Era managers operate. And just like what Central Station Era engineers did when they built power plants so big that they exploded, these managers are likely to inflict runaway Climate Chaos before they understand that they have reached a limit. Further, the regulations established by civil society to guide central station managers are designed to protect the central station paradigm by establishing and enforcing rules and regulations that either prohibit or make very difficult the formation of discrete, strategically-sized capital formations that, from a technology perspective, are eminently practical, but that would interfere with and diminish the market share of the electric utility services delivered by the central station paradigm.

It is statutes, rules and regulations, not any technological shortcomings, that are stunting the maturation of the Modern Era. For example, the City of Minneapolis has an interest in establishing its own municipal power authority because city residents want to rely on renewable energy much more than state law requires of Xcel Energy. Further, they want to purchase that renewable energy from tribal entities and other energy developers who utilize a community-based approach, as opposed to the community extraction process attached to projects developed by Xcel Energy. In addition, the community-based approach would be able to utilize existing transmission infrastructure to serve Minneapolis consumers, rather than requiring new transmission infrastructure as required by the Xcel Energy approach. But Minnesota statutes prevent the City of Minneapolis from establishing its own municipal power authority to accomplish these objectives because the city would be required to not only buy out the Xcel Energy infrastructure that serves customers within the city, but also to compensate Xcel shareholders for profits going forward into the future that Xcel shareholders would receive absent municipalization. We call it the "poison pill."

So on one hand the regulatory apparatus prevents Minneapolis energy consumers from taking full advantage of the economic, social and environmental benefits of municipalization. But on the other, statutes, rules and regulations require Xcel Energy ratepayers, including Minneapolis ratepayers, to pay for the billions of dollars' worth of new transmission infrastructure that Xcel Energy needs to deliver power from the remote wind and solar farms it has caused to be developed.

This contradiction reveals another aspect of the waning Central Station Era that must be overcome. Central Station players, whether they are Independent Power Producers or Investor Owned Utilities, are only attracted to energy projects that require very large capital formations, mostly because a nine to eleven percent return on an investment of a billion dollars is a lot more than a nien to eleven percent return on an investment of, say, $20 or $50 million. For monopoly central station players, smaller projects cost them more than they're worth, so they do not do them regardless of societal benefits. This means that regardless of economies of scale created by the *production* of the components of Modern Era technologies, the *deployment* of those components is required to mimic central station technologies before they are of any interest to central station players.

Hence the large remote wind and solar farms. Hence the need to get rules and regulations that make ratepayers pay for transmission infrastructure needed by remote wind and solar farms. By developing wind and solar projects in this manner, central station players are able to preserve the market share they have grown accustomed to enjoying during the Central Station Era, while deploying the renewable technologies of the Modern Era. And for central station players, it is all about market share. Because of their economies of scale during production, renewable energy technologies lend themselves perfectly to strategically sized projects that serve the local community in which they are located. We do not do such projects much yet because the rules and regulations are designed to guide and protect the owners of the increasingly obsolete central station paradigm machines.

Here is an interesting example of the dynamics in play as society tries to navigate the crosscurrents of the paradigm shift. Beginning around 2007, I decided that being as I had been working so hard for so long to improve the way in which electric utility services get delivered, I might as well see if I could develop our own 4.95 MW wind project for the North American Water Office. It took several years to find the right site, which needed to be somewhere within the region, have a good wind regime, be close enough to appropriately sized powerlines to transmit the electricity we would produce into the grid without requiring a prohibitively expensive substation, and it needed to be on land owned by someone willing to be a partner in developing the project. It turned out that the project wanted to be located on the top of a big hill out in a pasture in Haverhill Township about five miles northeast of Rochester, Minnesota. The site more than met all the conditions, and the excellent wind regime was good enough that we were projecting an annual capacity factor of forty percent. No new powerlines would be needed, because the size of the project would enable it to inject electricity into the sixty-nine kV powerline running past the property. The landowners were totally willing and excited and would be fifty-one percent owners of the project.

When Xcel Energy put out a "request for proposals" early in 2013, we responded with our formal offer of the Haverhill Project with a purchase price of $0.03/kWh for the power the project would produce. Xcel rejected our proposal because its cut-off rate turned out to be $0.029/kWh, so we missed it by *that* much. Turned out, of course, that while Xcel's 2013 Request for Proposals scored several hundred megawatts of power at or below its $0.029 limit, all of the projects it accepted were located much further west where annual wind speeds are slightly higher than we had at Haverhill, but they all required new transmission infrastructure in order to deliver the power to market. Those transmission requirements amounted to several hundred million dollars, but transmission costs were externalized from the bidding process because they would cost Xcel Energy nothing. Ratepayers paid them.

The consequences of this unearned subsidy given to central station players is staggering. Our little 4.95 MW project would produce on the order of 17,000 MWH per year, and the value of that electricity at $0.03/kWh is over $520,000 per year. That cash-flow would pay the $8,422,009 cost of the project over time, with revenue exceeding costs by about $2,000,000 over a projected twenty year lifespan for the project. There are opportunities to develop literally thousands of similar strategically sized projects throughout the Upper Midwest, if harvesting renewable energy resources at a community scale were the objective. The combined wealth such projects would produce amounts to billions of dollars per year, wealth that would serve interests within the communities where the power was generated, where it would circulate many times over. Instead, this potential community wealth gets siphoned off to serve private interests of central station managers and shareholders. This type of thievery should not be tolerated, let alone normalized.

REA G&T systems have their own way of ensuring the economic success of the big central station power plants they own and operate, even while the paradigm shifts. They use "all requirements" contracts. These contracts require the G&T's member distribution coops to purchase all, or some specified big number like ninety-five percent of all the electricity they sell to their consumer members, from their G&T electricity provider regardless of cost. The distribution coop isn't allowed to capture the value of the wind and the sun in their own neighborhoods and communities because then it wouldn't be buying enough electricity from the G&T to support operations at their big central station plant. This type of management does not seem reasonable, equitable or sustainable.

Even as the Central Station Era slowly phases out, society is still learning about how to regulate central station electric utilities with standards and requirements so they are less destructive of public interests. After a slow start, it took until 1963 to enact the Clean Air Act, and that was mostly for soot. The acids in the stack gases did not get the attention they deserved until the mid-1980s, after the Adirondack Mountains started dissolving. Measures to manage the metals smelted out of central station coal fires finally began to get implemented sometime after that, and we remain ineffectual regarding carbon dioxide, the dominant greenhouse gas. Then there's all the methane that is still leaking at natural gas extraction sites, unresolved problems with nuclear waste, and failure to manage routine and accidental radiation releases from commercial nuclear reactors. The job of proper regulation of central station power companies remains a work in progress.

Nonetheless, over time, standards were adopted in attempts to manage and control these situations created by the manner in which society delivered electric utility services. Setting standards became the conventional tool society used to get power companies to act more in accordance with public interests. So shortly after the turn of the new century, as the climate situation started coming into focus for those who were paying attention, it was quite natural for legislators and regulators and a whole lot of enviros to attempt to use Renewable Energy Standards (RES) as the tool to get central station players to reduce their major and continuing contribution to the escalating ravages of Climate Chaos. In Minnesota, a renewable energy standard was passed by the legislature in 2007. As of this writing, the state is somewhere around thirty-one percent in terms of in state electrical production, and is scheduled to be at fifty-five percent by 2035, assuming we still have a functional society at that time.

The problem, of course, is that in order to make a difference, very large amounts of renewable energy must come online quickly to displace fossil fuel combustion. Considering the nature of this problem, and how we can literally watch the accelerating effects of Climate Chaos every day of our lives, taking twenty-eight years, from 2007 to 2035, to reach a bit over half seems remarkably passive. By happenstance or by design, a feature of this timeline is that it will allow central station utilities to wring every last cent out of their existing fleet of fossil fuel generators before they retire. It also provides time for construction of transmission required for the massive, remote wind and solar farms that consumers will get snookered into buying for IOU shareholders and managers. And people living in communities where the power-lines come from, where the wealth produced by harvesting renewable energy resources simply gets extracted, have demonstrated a tendency to offer resistance to renewable energy because, like the farmer said, "If they ain't your pigs, it just stinks like pig shit."

These factors combine to make RES rather ineffectual, a conclusion reinforced by the increased incidents of havoc-reeking natural phenomenon that we are all experiencing.

Some of us recognized these shortcomings at the time, and we did our best to offer an alternative approach. We called it C-BED, Community-Based Energy Development. We got a law passed by the 2005 Minnesota Legislature that set up a process for qualifying C-BED projects to negotiate Power Purchase Agreements with electric utilities. The idea was to spur development of thousands of small, dispersed utility-scale projects distributed throughout the state, and owned by people in the community where the C-BED project was located. Our intent was to provide a foundation for economic democracy.

It did not work. Some years later, the C-BED statute was rescinded. What we learned, among other things, was to not allow corporations intent on killing your initiative in on the negotiations that determine the conditions by which your initiative will operate. C-BED died a painful death.

We also learned how complicated and money-biased it is to secure the Interconnection Agreement that allows your project to get connected to the ISO regulated grid. We learned about a host of Byzantine financial instruments, like passive income tax credits, that make it difficult for people in their own communities to secure the financing needed to develop a utility-scale project. But we also began to understand how to accelerate the pace of the paradigm shift from central station to the Modern Era by getting more strategic about how to size and site utility-scale renewable generation facilities.

It is also true that technology advances can produce unexpected results. Take "advanced reconductoring" for example. Reconductoring has good potential to significantly reduce costs for providing new high-voltage transmission capacity. But even with reconductoring, new high-voltage transmission capacity will still cost a lot of money. Meanwhile, the cost to transmit baseload power generated within each load-serving substation to consumers within that footprint will be zero, because it will all get consumed within the footprint.

# Chapter 4
## On the Demand Side

The reason why the electric utility industry sells kilowatt hours of electricity is because that is what it produces. In most industries, selling the product that you produce would be normal, and as things should be. Such a business model is most certainly good enough for electric utility managers, shareholders, regulators including judges, politicians that set the law for the regulators and judges, and virtually all electric utility customers along with just about everybody else. It requires no thought: power companies generate and sell kilowatt hours of electricity. It's what they do.

It would be really helpful if everybody who thinks like this were to pause long enough to consider what it is that electric utilities actually *do* for society.

A person can *look* at the stuff most companies sell. Except, maybe, some of the spiritual stuff. People have some sort of a relationship with the stuff most companies sell to them, including the spiritual stuff.

Ever had a relationship with a kilowatt-hour? What might that feel like? Have you ever seen one?

The fact of the matter is that when you pay your electric bill, what you have actually purchased are functions and services that you need and/or desire. What you want is for the darkness to vanish when you flip the switch. You want your food to remain fresh and edible longer than it would if you left it sitting on the table. You want to see a movie or watch the news to learn about the latest calamities caused by Climate Chaos and all the warring. You want all the electric motors to do their jobs and the conveyor belts to keep on turning. What you want is the joy of cooking. What you want is *not* a bunch of kilowatt hours of electricity, and if that were what you had, you would have no idea what to do with them, except to maybe drop them before you got hurt. Without end use devices, kilowatt hours are of no use to you. Kilowatt hours are simply the medium that delivers an end use function or provides you with some service.

In the beginning of the electrical era, this distinction regarding the conceptualized nature of electrical energy did not matter much because end use functions that electricity could perform were rather limited. Lighting and electric motors performed a quickly expanding array of jobs, but still, mostly lights and motors. That's why many electric companies had "Light & Power" in their name. With only a relatively few end use functions to perform, and quaint amounts of electricity required to perform them, there were no serious and immediate consequences created by confusing the medium for the product, and so the confusion persisted while the size and scope of end use functions rapidly expanded. As electrical energy markets continued growing, so did this persistent confusion, but the difference between the medium and the product remained an abstract distinction that made no apparent difference to anyone. It became so totally normal to sell electricity as a commodity that the distinction was not recognized as a foundational flaw. It was not until 1976, in the wake of the Arab Oil Embargo, that Amory Lovins of the Rocky Mountain Institute coined the phrase "soft energy path" and actually examined the relationship between the commodity that power companies were selling and the functional reasons why electrical energy consumers were purchasing it.

So, the fact is that power companies sell a commodity while consumers purchase services and functions, and this is called a "contradiction." It's a contradiction because power supplier interests get served when they generate and sell more kilowatt hours of electricity, while consumer and societal interests are served by performing the desired functions and services as efficiently as possible, with the least amount of electricity. But this contradiction remains largely unrecognized, and so the confusion persists to this day.

Selling a commodity means that for power companies, revenues increase as more of their commodity product gets sold. Whether we're talking about IOUs, or REA Cooperatives, or municipal power authorities, they sell kWhs, and the more of them they sell, the better their financial health. It's basic. The more electricity any specific power company generates and/or sells, the healthier will be the financial status of that power company. The more it sells, the more revenue it will have available to manage its business. Conversely, energy conservation, by definition, decreases energy sales and therefore, absent regulatory interference, also reduces revenue flowing to the seller/producer of the electric commodity.

We previously discussed the way in which an electric utility rate-case proceeds. The system is regulated so that if the utility sells all the electricity it forecasts it would sell in its "test year," it will meet its designated, regulated rate-of-return, and all expenses are covered. If it sells more than the forecast amount, all the revenue produced by selling the additional electricity is bonus money, because all the expenses were already covered by revenue generated as it sold the forecast amount. Except for the added fuel, and there's the fuel adjustment clause for that. When sales exceed expectations, shareholders line up for a bonus dividend. Conversely, electric utility financial health declines when energy sales fail to meet "test year" expectations.

REA and municipal managers like to say how they serve their members, not distant shareholders, and how all revenues are put into the service of their member-consumers, "So do not go accusing us of seeking profits," they proclaim. And it is true that REA systems and municipal districts, when managed properly, manage revenue from energy sales to serve the interests of their community members instead of siphoning that wealth off to satisfy greedy shareholders, or maybe a coal company. The point remains, however, that increased revenues due to increased sales of electricity increases the financial well-being of all electric utilities. Increased sales means increased electrical energy production. Increased energy production means more fossil fuel combustion and more combustion waste gasses, and if reactors are involved, the production of more nuclear waste, including high-level nuclear waste that no one knows how to isolate from biological activity, as is required for the next 240,000 years or so.

In other words, electric utility business models punish business practices that reduce the electric utility industry's contribution to ecological degradation, and reward business practices that increase the industry's contribution to ecological degradation, including the amount of greenhouse gas emissions injected into the atmosphere. This is backward. *Society rewards power companies financially for emitting the pollution responsible for Climate Chaos, but regulated power companies must be ordered to manage energy conservation programs that reduce the pollution.* In fact, it was not until about a year *after* NAWO demonstrated the pollution control value of energy conservation during Minnesota's Acid Deposition Control Act proceedings, that NSP was ordered to produce its very first Conservation Improvement Plan (CIP), which it submitted to the Minnesota Public Utilities Commission on May 1, 1987, and then the commission issued its first CIP order on January 5, 1988.

But how well do *you* do things that you really don't want to do, but are ordered to do anyway? While the idea of energy conservation was finally entering public consciousness as something positive, conservation programs, understandably, did a poor job of actually saving energy. How poorly? We'll get to that directly.

For decades, of course, the primary strategy for dealing with Climate Chaos was ignorance that then got cloaked in denial, but in due course, it became apparent that such strategies were not working very well. So then, beginning in Berlin in 1995, as the consequences of Climate Chaos accelerated and the need to take corrective actions became increasingly apparent, our collective global society decided to gather every few years for a big conference to talk about it. Global leaders continue jet-setting around the world to extravagant venues every few years, where they mostly point fingers and argue as to who is at fault for the ravaging destruction, and who should pay how much in damages. With so much privilege at stake, these global leaders remain mostly trapped in a paralyzing and unsightly blame game. Meanwhile, with some exceptions that time will tell, strategies to remediate escalating consequences remain largely ineffectual if not merely aspirational. That's pretty much where we are at as of this writing.

By now, however, there's been enough of the ravaging destruction so that global civil society, such as it is, has been compelled to grapple with the fact that extracting fossil fuels and burning them is driving Climate Chaos. Unfortunately, we waited long enough so that there are now multiple drivers. There's melting permafrost releasing methane gas that had been locked into the frozen Arctic earth for eons. This will increasingly come in big bubbles and burps, as well as a slower, constant release to the atmosphere. Methane traps heat about eighty times as effectively as does carbon dioxide, and we may well be already on the brink of a runaway greenhouse condition. Let's not dwell on that. But there's also deforestation, which causes trees to remove less carbon dioxide from the atmosphere, while many surviving forests dry out, and then burning wildfires add their contribution. Feedback loops are now becoming evident as ocean currents slow, the distribution of energy absorbed by our atmospheric blanket with its methane and carbon dioxide slows, and increased heat/energy in the biosphere leads to ever more violent and extreme weather and climate conditions. Bigger storms. Larger weather patterns containing much more energy. Atmospheric rivers. When was the first time you heard about "atmospheric rivers?" Melting polar ice and rising sea levels. Stalled out ocean currents will soon become the subject of major public discussions.

Our situation is dire. On February 8, 2024, Copernicus, the European Union's climate and weather monitoring service, reported that a primary benchmark has been reached. Previously, at a big climate conference in 2015, the Paris Agreement was adopted, which established the objective of limiting the amount of global warming to no more than 1.5° C above the pre-industrial average. On February 8, Copernicus announced that the average 2023 global temperature reached 1.52° C above the pre-industrial average, and that the trend line was accelerating in the wrong direction. The global average temperature for January 2024 was 1.66° C above the pre-industrial average and during that month, average global sea temperatures were the hottest on record, beating the previous record by 0.26° Celsius, which is A LOT, considering the mass and density of the oceans compared to the atmosphere. The first eight days of February 2024 were the hottest on record. As of this writing, the world is now in it's tenth straight month of highest monthly average temperatures on record. Copernicus called out fossil fuel combustion as the culprit.

Anyway, it is generally recognized that dramatically reducing carbon dioxide emissions caused by fossil fuel combustion to the atmosphere is essential if the worst consequences of the Climate Chaos Crisis are to be avoided. But doing so is perceived to be expensive. For those captains of industry who manage large energy corporations that make decisions about how the global economy, as well as countries and smaller jurisdictions meet their energy needs, the required dramatic reductions in fossil fuel combustion will cost them a lot of money and result in profound reductions of incoming revenues to which they are accustomed. Regardless of whether or not these corporations diversify, they will lose market share if they are not put out of business, and to them, that is unacceptable. They cannot help themselves. The global order, such as it is, will crash and burn before corporate energy extractors and managers and oligarchs of various stripes will voluntarily allow their market share to be purposefully reduced or eliminated. For better or worse, there are no actors on the global stage who are big enough and strong enough, or informed and motivated enough, to force them to change their business model, regardless of global consequences. At least not yet. Maybe those little acorns can grow to become metaphoric.

Fortunately, in a perverse way, electric utility contributions to Climate Chaos are large enough so that remediation strategies might make a difference. Equally important, electric utility regulatory structures provide at least an opportunity for reform. For instance, what if the electric utility reward structure caused the financial health of power companies to depend on the efficient use of its product, rather than on its consumption, including its wasteful consumption? Or what if power company consumers were given an opportunity to purchase more efficient end use devices by paying for their purchase over time on their monthly energy bill, which incorporated the value of the energy conserved to pay off the debt on the more efficient device? What if we compensated power suppliers by using financial structures that rewarded the behavior we need to reduce the destruction, instead of using financial structures that reward it?

To understand the difference that could be made by instituting proper incentives for electric utility managers, one needs to know a bit about the technical potential to save electricity, and a bit more about electric utility energy and capacity forecasting.

Historically, and mostly to this day, power companies use "econometric" forecasts. In essence, econometric forecasters look at historical trend lines, make a few adjustments if they know about a few new factories coming online or an old one shutting down, make a few more adjustments to account for demographic changes, and use those numbers to recalibrate the most recent energy and capacity requirements for the "base year" of their forecast. Then they decide if they are growing at three percent or whatever and do the math. There's your forecast. It's a projection that presumes continued exponential growth, and that has limited value in terms of helping to guide the management of the electrical loads that it projects. The objective of economic forecasting is to enable utility managers to build enough new electrical generation capacity fast enough to stay ahead of the curve.

Econometric forecasting was developed during an era of exponential growth in the electric utility industry. It assumes and projects exponential growth through the forecast period. Exponential growth, however, has a doubling time. For example, a two percent/yr. growth rate will cause a doubling every thirty-five years. At seven percent, it is just ten years. The point is that exponential growth in finite systems, such as our Earth, has an end to it. It is not sustainable. There are limits to growth, as The Club of Rome published in 1972, and when those limits are reached, systems collapse. Even intuitively, therefore, it would seem to be imprudent to manage earthly natural resources such as fossil fuels and radioactive substances, with a tool that is at odds with this reality. Econometric forecasting is a passive tool that leads to self-fulfilling prophesies and vicious cycles because after presuming that percent per year system growth rates will deviate only marginally from the historical trend, electric utility management is then responsible for building electrical generation infrastructure to meet that system-wide projected trend of exponential growth, and then management is responsible for enabling the growth in electrical demand required for optimum use of the infrastructure required by the projected growth. And by then it is time for another forecast. Such management is not good for the situation in which we find ourselves.

End Use Analysis offers an alternative approach to electric utility management.

Electrical end use analysis was developed by the Rocky Mountain Institute around 1980 and first introduced to the Minnesota electric utility crowd by TKO during our intervention against Sherco 3. Evidence and testimony presented by TKO clearly demonstrated that a robust energy conservation program informed by end use analysis would eliminate the need for Sherco 3 at a dramatically lower cost than building Sherco 3. But of course, the power companies and their buddies in state government were having none of that, as the lot of them had not yet even begun to think about, let alone understand the value of programs that would systematically enable electricity to be used more efficiently. Their Certificate of Need proceedings are designed to demonstrate that proposed projects *are* needed, and they are good at doing so in significant part because the rate structure rewards power companies for selling kWhs, not saving them. And the only way to keep on selling more kWhs. is to keep on building more power plants. So TKO got beat.

Nonetheless, the value of this end use methodology stuck in the minds of some of the bureaucratic lesserlings at the time. Years later, in 1988, when these lesserlings had moved up the ladder a bit at the Department of Public Service, they remembered the analysis TKO had provided, and conducted the first and only End Use Analysis for the State of Minnesota. They published its methodology and findings in a Department of Public Service document entitled "Minnesota's Energy Options for the 1990s." Then all three of them got fired at the same time very shortly thereafter, and the DPS got restructured into the Department of Commerce.

*This analysis concluded that the total Minnesota electrical energy conservation technical potential was fifty-two percent.* In other words, according to the Minnesota Department of Public Service, we were wasting over half of all the kWhs of electricity consumed in Minnesota by using uncontrolled motors, inefficient appliances and lighting systems, and other wasteful end use devices. Needless to say, after firing the three up and coming lesserlings, state authorities did their best to erase the information and neither the State nor the utilities have ever done another end use analysis ever since. However, more sophisticated end use analysis conducted by the Rocky Mountain Institute in that same timeframe put the national technical potential for energy conservation closer to a whopping seventy-five percent. Consider: one and a half percent to two percent of annual revenue required to be spent on Conservation Improvement Plans, compared to a fifty percent to seventy-five percent energy savings potential. That's how poorly.

End Use Analysis breaks out each electrical end use for each of the economic sectors which are the industrial, commercial, residential and agriculture. There's also another category to account for public sector and governmental energy consumption. The analysis then identifies the percentage of the total electrical load consumed by each end-use, sector by sector. For example, one break-out is residential refrigerators, which in 1988 used 5.9 percent of all electricity consumed in Minnesota. Another example is commercial lighting, which used 14.1 percent of all electricity consumed. Another is industrial motors which used 19.8 percent. Residential dishwashers used 0.3 percent. Commercial ventilation used 2.9 percent. All told, a good end use analysis accounts for the entire load of a given area, be it a state, nation, or power company service territory, and breaks out over thirty specific end uses, covering all sectors.

After accounting for all existing electrical consumption, you go to work and identify the most energy efficient, commercially available end use devices that perform each of the end use functions that are broken out in the analysis. For example, the most efficient commercially available refrigerator used only about twenty percent of the electricity required by the average refrigerator that was in use at that time, meaning that a systematic program to replace old, inefficient refrigerators with high-efficiency new ones would reduce residential refrigerator electrical consumption by a prodigious eighty percent. There is no data suggesting that average refrigerator electrical consumption has improved that much since 1990, and now that ice makers are common, any refrigerator efficiency improvements since 1990 are marginal. In Minnesota, that improvement alone would amount to displacing about 500 megawatts of generating capacity, which is well over half of all the power that Sherco 3 generates, and it would have reduced Minnesota's overall electrical energy requirement by over four percent. By comparing how much electricity is consumed by existing devices being used, to the amount of electricity that would be consumed if the most efficient commercially available end use devices were performing those same functions, utility managers would gain the ability to not only *forecast* future requirements, but to also

*manage* each specific end use load so that total future energy requirements fall within specific, articulated goals with far more sophistication than conventional load-management tools.

For example, staying with refrigerators, utility regulators and/or
utility management would inventory, with as much specificity as possible, the amount of refrigeration capacity and the age of refrigeration
units in its service territory, neighborhood by neighborhood, business
by business, block by block and then house by house. With the information this inventory provides, the Refrigeration Efficiency Program
of the utility would design and implement its program to systematically replace, on an ongoing basis, older less efficient refrigerators with
new, high-efficiency refrigerators. Of course, no one would be *required*
to get a new refrigerator, but a well-designed and managed refrigerator
efficiency program could enable every household that gets an electric
bill to pay for their nice, new, energy efficient refrigerator over time,
as they pay their *reduced* electric bill. Their bill would be reduced, obviously, because their nice, new energy efficient refrigerator would be
using less electricity than their old clunker.

With detailed knowledge about each end use for each sector, utility
managers would be able to provide their customers with electric utility services that are much more equitable, far more efficient and with
much less pollution. Further, it turns out that it would be a lot cheaper
from a societal perspective to guide the delivery of electric utility services with policy based on managing end uses than it is to build the new
supply-side infrastructure that is required to power all the unmanaged,
inefficient end use devices that are in service and still being sold. Doing
so would also produce a lot more better-paying jobs in business sectors
having to do with the manufacturing, sales, and installation of refrigerators and water heaters and motor controls and air conditioning and
lighting and ventilation and heat pump systems and cooking and all the
other urgently needed energy efficiency improvements.

Market penetration of high-efficiency end use devices may have
accelerated a bit since the 1988 Minnesota Department of Public Ser-

vice end use analysis, just as it is also possible that technologies that improve energy efficiency are advancing in today's world at a faster rate than they were back then but penetrate the market no faster than they did in 1988. Maybe someone should do an end use analysis to find out which it is. If the former is true, today's technical potential to improve energy efficiency is somewhat less than fifty-two percent. If the latter is true, the gap between actual performance and the technical potential has risen above the fifty-two percent mark. Either way, end use efficiency improvement opportunities abound.

Take lighting, for example. In 1988, incandescent light bulbs still dominated the market, but screw-in fluorescent bulbs were available, and they did the lighting job as well as incandescent light bulbs. But they used only $1/10^{th}$ the wattage to produce a the same amount of lumens as their incandescent competitor. Light Emitting Diode (LED) technology was still in the lab back then, but now LEDs are readily available and use only $1/10^{th}$ the wattage per lumen as fluorescent lights. So undoubtedly, the amount of electricity consumed by lighting in all sectors now is different than it was in 1988, and the technical potential to improve lighting efficiency is also different. Unfortunately, there is no analysis available that would enable energy managers to understand, on a system-wide basis, the value of an end use efficiency improvement program focused on lighting.

Likewise with commercial and industrial electric motors. In 1988, motor controls that would allow a motor to use only as much electricity as the load required were becoming available. So instead of being either "off" or "on," a controlled elevator motor would use much less electricity to lift just a couple people than if the elevator were full. How many uncontrolled or poorly controlled electric motors are still powering commerce and industry? Who knows?

Residential clothes washers and dryers provide an up-to-date example of the opportunity that rate designs with proper incentive structures can create to save consumers money, while reducing environmental destruction. GRIST reported on February 29, 2024, that the federal government has established new standards that will increase the energy efficiency of these appliances. The GRIST article reported that residential washers and dryers account for eight percent of household electrical consumption, and that the new standards, which will become effective March 1st, 2028, will reduce electric consumption for washing machines by eight percent and also use twenty-eight percent less water, and dryers will use forty percent less electricity. These energy efficiency improvements will, GRIST reports, reduce the average household energy bill by $120 per year, and over a thirty year period, save energy consumers $2.2 billion while reducing $CO_2$ emissions by seventy-one million tons.

This GRIST report demonstrates once again, about thirty-five years after the lesserlings got fired for it, the public interest value of end use analysis. But the reason why the federal government had to set these standards is that incentive structures for delivering electric utility services cause power company revenues to decline when the high-efficiency washers and dryers get installed. This depresses market penetration of the pollution reducing, consumer saving appliances. If, however, clever humans were to adjust their stupid electric utility incentive structure, power companies would invest directly to purchase high-efficiency washers and dryers. They would get a regulated return on their investment, consumer electric bills would be reduced, there would be more well-paying washer/dryer manufacturing jobs in the overall economy, and pollution would get abated. Further, as the high-efficiency appliances get installed, electrical generation requirements of the power company would be reduced accordingly. And the value of the electrical generation capacity no longer consumed by the old, *in*efficient washers and dryers that got retired would be *less* than the cost of purchasing *new* electrical generation capacity. In other words, in addition to all the other benefits of correcting this hideous flaw in our economic structure, electric utility managers would gain a valuable tool for managing their electrical loads more strategically and cost-effectively as they balance supply and demand side requirements.

Heat pumps, whether ground or air sourced, provide another example. Heat pump technology barely existed in 1988 but is a readily available technology today and provides a much more efficient technology for space conditioning. What is the technical potential of heat pumps to improve energy efficiency across all sectors? An end use analysis would enable energy managers to understand this potential and design programs that could profoundly reduce the amount of energy used for space conditioning.

On a slightly different tack, there are electrical end uses today that did not exist in 1988. One of them is transportation. Electric vehicle sales are surging, driven in significant part by the growing realization that fossil fuel combustion threatens civilization, such as it is. This raises a question about all those charging stations: How marginal does the benefit of electric vehicles become when they are powered by coal plants and fission reactors? Another new end use that did not exist in 1988 has to do with the "cloud," which, of course, is not a cloud. Presently, it's somewhere around 9,000 - 11,000 industrial buildings around the world that store selfies and spreadsheets and other bits of vital information while consuming prodigious amounts of energy. They must be cooled, which can lead to water issues, and energy and capacity requirements for this new end use are growing rapidly. As requirements for data management and artificial intelligence ramp up, they are likely to counter-balance, if not overwhelm, whatever energy savings can be achieved by increasing the efficiency of other end uses. The cosmic joke will be complete when human intelligence creates artificial intelligence that transforms enough fossil fuel into pollution to drive Earth's life sustaining ecosystems into chaos. Perhaps a first step back from the brink would be a global agreement to power "cloud" infrastructure with, and only with, up to date space conditioning technologies and renewable energy and energy storage systems, thereby providing a legitimate application of renewable energy technologies mimicking the central station paradigm. Or maybe fusion technology will save the day.

In any event, whether the rate of market penetration of high-efficiency end use devices has increased since 1988 despite the financial disincentive utility managers have to promote such technologies, or if instead, the rate of efficiency improvements of end use technologies has increased faster than market penetration rates of such technologies since 1988, consider the magnitude of the wealth that utility managers and regulators were able to extract from ratepayers during the past thirty-five years or so, because their management was not guided by end use analysis. In big round numbers, total electrical consumption in the United States between 1990 and 2023 was in the ballpark of 120 trillion kWh, around three trillion kWh in 1990, up to over 4 trillion kWh in 2023. Presume that the market penetration rate of high-efficiency technologies remained relatively constant over that period of time, as there were no power company policies or practices that would cause it to increase. Then, if the conservation improvement potential remained around the fifty percent mark identified by Minnesota's bureaucratic lesserlings in 1988, at an average price of $0.10/kWh between 1988 and 2023, power company interests walked off with somewhere around $6 trillion of ratepayer money during those years. At an average price of $0.12/kWh, that would be $7.2 trillion. As the electric utility industry and its regulators have failed to conduct analyses that would produce a more robust conclusion, feel free to put your own "+ & -" bounds on it. But ask yourself: how much better would you feel about this wealth extraction if it were only $2 trillion over those thirty-five years, instead of $6 or $7 trillion?

How many billions of metric tons of carbon dioxide injected into the atmosphere do you think are attached to $6 trillion worth of electricity? Well, in 2022, according to the US Energy Information Administration, electricity from all energy sources was responsible for 1.65 billion metric tons of carbon, which equates to 0.86 lb./kWh. If end use analysis had been driving "least-cost" energy development since 1990 and achieving the fifty percent mark identified in the 1988 Minnesota analysis, the $6 trillion it would have saved ratepayers between then and now would translate into a reduction of 51,600,000,000,000 metric tons of carbon dioxide in Earth's atmosphere. That's enough, arguably, to make a difference. Or at least maybe it might have been.

The necessary questions, then, from a public interest perspective, have to do with why are power company managers and regulators allowed to be so jaded, decade after decade, that they can discard this awesome analytical tool while enriching themselves and driving civilized society, such as it is, toward an ecological holocaust? Just think about this for a minute: global climate apocalypse caused significantly by electric utility pollution is well underway; that pollution is at apocalyptic levels because society simply wastes most of the electricity it consumes; society financially rewards electric utilities for promoting the wasteful consumption and protects their financial security by providing them with monopoly status; and, for more than thirty years, despite the escalating crisis and knowledge about how to resolve the contradiction, society refuses to correct electric utility rate design flaws that are driving human civilization toward catastrophe. How's that for thuggish stupidity?

To be fair, in May of 2015 the MN Public Utilities Commission finally and formally recognized this terrible flaw in its rate design and approved a pilot program for NSP's residential and small business consumers that de-coupled the direct connection between power company revenues and energy sales. Not surprisingly, however, the pilot failed to attach NSP's earnings to investments into increased energy efficiency, which, after all, is the whole point. When they ended the program in 2019 and did a "revenue true-up," it turned out that NSP got to sock residential and small business customers an additional 0.3 cents per kWh to make up for its revenue shortfall. How's that for thuggishly stupid perverts?

There are many ways to properly correct this terrible flaw. We have already touched on one, called Inclusive Financing or On-Bill Financing, some version of which has been adopted by several smaller municipal and REA jurisdictions around the country, and which has been struggling, so far unsuccessfully, to gain acceptance in Minnesota for almost a decade. For more on this struggle, visit the Community Power website at www.communitypowermn.org.

Inclusive Financing can be applied to gas as well as electric utilities and is driven by the obvious and easy to understand fact that energy efficiency improvements cause energy consumers to save money on their energy bill. The idea is to establish a pool of capital through legislation or regulation that is strategically sized to match the needs of the jurisdiction. This pool of capital can be managed by a utility, or some other entity created by legislation or regulation. Energy customers draw on this pool of capital for money to purchase qualifying, high-efficiency end use devices and pay back the capital pool over time as they pay their energy bill. Everybody gets included on the deal, because a portion of the money saved by the efficiency improvement stays with the consumer as the reward for making the improvement, and the other portion of the money saved goes back to the capital pool to pay off the debt.

In a more enlightened setting, a bit of overhead could be eliminated by enabling the utility itself to finance the end use efficiency improvement with an appropriate rate-of-return on the pool of capital it establishes for the purpose of financing the improvements. In fact, CenterPoint Energy, the Minneapolis gas utility that Community Power has been working with to establish Inclusive Financing for Minneapolis natural gas consumers, offered to host and manage the capital pool, and it seemed we were on track to break new ground with a high-profile Inclusive Financing program. But before we could get it to go, CenterPoint pulled a bait-and-switch by unilaterally jacking the interest rate on the capital pool to a prohibitive level and at least for now, once again the effort fell apart with another demonstration of the actual nature of greedy bastards running most energy utility companies.

Another way to correct the flaw that rewards power companies for polluting by selling more electricity would be to establish a variable rate-of-return on the utility rate-base. This would be similar to what I got NSP to do with its little conservation program back in the late 1980s. But instead of just applying the variable rate-of-return to the minuscule conservation portion of the rate-base, it would be applied to the entire rate-base. The baseline rate-of-return on the power company's entire rate-base would be set low, perhaps in the range of two to three percent, and that is where it would stay unless and until the utility demonstrates that its energy efficiency improvement investments were producing measurable results. Then, as the power company demonstrated that its investments into demand side improvements increased end use energy efficiency, the carrot side of this stick would increase the rate-of-return on the entire rate-base according to benchmarks that could be specified, end use by end use. This type of rate design would encourage proactive conservation management practices designed to maximize the rate-of-return on the entire rate-base, which would in turn produce a much more balanced supply-side/demand-side portfolio. Adjustments to the rate-of-return on the entire rate-base could also be used to encourage energy efficiency simply by allowing the rate-of-return to rise as *fewer* kilowatt hours get sold, while still holding the power company accountable for all performance standards regarding reliability, pollution control and so forth. Over time, true-up mechanisms applied to the variable rate-of-return approach would ensure that the power company was rewarded for socially responsible behavior and punished financially for misbehaving.

Energy intensity offers another approach to rate reform. Energy intensity is a measure of the energy efficiency of an economy. It is calculated as units of energy per unit of GDP (gross domestic product) or some other measure of economic output. Minnesota utility managers and regulators got a brief taste of an Energy Intensity rate model after NSP built Sherco 3. By the late 1980s, the time had come for ratepayers to begin paying for it, and in this rate case, NAWO developed and presented for the record an "Energy Intensity" model. Energy intensity is routinely measured by economists for a variety of purposes, and it tells you how much energy, electricity, in this case, is used to provide all the goods and services consumed within a given geographic area. Conventionally, that area is a state or nation, but it could be an electric utility's service territory. The Energy Intensity model would cause the rate-of-return on the electric utility's investment into its rate-base, the infrastructure it owns and operates to provide electric utility services, to increase at a regulated rate as it demonstrates that the infrastructure in which it invests reduces the amount of electricity needed to provide a given set of goods and services within its service territory. The model is on the record but was rejected with the excuse that nobody knows how to measure energy intensity as a function of economic activity within an electric utility service territory. Never mind that humans have an uncanny ability to measure any kaflutin thing they want to measure, including wobbles in the gravitational space/time continuum originating on the far side of the Universe billions of years before our sun flashed to fusion. A few years later (after the Sherco 3 rate-case, not the sun's ignition) NSP adopted my performance-based approach to its conservation program.

Waiting around for individual energy consumers, be they households, or business enterprises or even major industries, to invest in high-efficiency end use devices means that market penetration rates for these technologies will not deviate much from historical trends. Due to economic disparities and a multitude of distractions, households are slow to respond to technology improvements, but the situation is even worse, on average, with rental households, where flawed incentive structures often make it more profitable for apartment owners to put cheap, inefficient appliances in their units, seeing as the renters pay the electric bill. Even though most energy efficiency improvements for business and industry go straight to their bottom-line, energy management is usually no more than a secondary concern because they are in business primarily to do their business, which is something other than providing for their energy services.

The gap between the technical potential to improve energy efficiency and the actual performance of electric utility conservation programs creates opportunities for an assortment of non-utility professional energy services providers, similar to what usually happens when low performance collides with high potential in the marketplace. Some of these businesses contract with a power company so that CIP requirements get met, and the business of others is to capture the value of energy that would otherwise be wasted due to inefficient end use management. While such businesses should certainly be profitable, they have not done much to close the gap between actual performance and the technical potential to use energy more efficiently.

So it gets back to proper incentives. What do we reward? There are many electric utility rate designs that semi-rational humans of average intelligence ought to be able to deploy so that humanity does not stew in its own extremely profitable wastes. We do not use common sense electric utility rate designs only because doing so would interfere with privileges presently served when increasing energy consumption is rewarded financially, and because most energy consumers are functionally illiterate when it comes to energy management. Do you recall the difference between a kilowatt-hour and a megawatt?

Now here we are, stuck in the stew. But environmental concerns aside, what would be the consequences of rational electric utility management that was rewarded for delivering energy services efficiently, instead of doing it backward? Good question.

So far, we have been examining the demand side of the electric utility equation. Before we can talk meaningfully about what it means to get energy right, we must also examine the supply side of the matter. We'll do that next.

# Chapter 5

When we get energy right, should that actually occur, we'll be able to do what needs doing because we'll have the energy. But there are two sides of it, not counting politics: the demand side, and the supply side. We have examined extensive and compelling information about derangement on the demand side of delivering energy services, what with rewarding anti-social behavior and all, and what to do about it. Now we will look at the supply side.

The Central Station Era isn't over, but it's mostly just a question of how much more damage the massive custom built power plants will inflict before most of them are retired and replaced by end use efficiency improvements, renewable energy and energy storage technologies. This eventuality got reinforced again by federal Environmental Protection Agency on April 25, 2024, with the adoption of rules that require coal plants to capture and sequester ninety percent of their carbon emissions by 2039, even though most of the remaining coal plants will have been shuttered by then anyway. Maybe by then some form of hydrogen fusion will become commercially available, but for the meanwhile, the big custom-built central station power plants have become too expensive and take too long to build relative to the competition emerging from renewable energy and energy storage technologies, to say nothing of the potential for demand side improvements, if only we were somehow able to get our incentives properly adjusted.

Certainly, however, it is not the ecological destruction caused by waste from central station generators that is driving the transition to renewables. If it were, the recent EPA rule would be calling for carbon sequestration immediately, and a similar rule promulgated over a decade ago by the Obama administration would not have been rescinded by the MAGA Spanky Trump debacle. Even though the cost of carbon does get litigated from time to time, mostly by young people who foresee a desperate future, the world order, such as it is, will be shredded to pieces and torched before a compelling moral or ecological purpose overcomes the privileges of power brokers and their sycophants. Rather, emerging economics provide the driving force for the energy transition, and the environment gets to come along for the ride.

Not counting pollution, renewable energy and energy storage technologies have three attributes that give them competitive advantages which make them insurmountable in a fair fight. All their components are mass-produced, so the more components you make, the cheaper each discrete unit of electrical generation becomes. Therefore, you want to make lots and lots of them, and then you want to keep on making more until some future saturation point. Second, renewable energy generation and storage projects are modular, which means that any particular project can be as large or as small as you want it to be, all things considered. This versatility allows for human intelligence, such as it is, to drive the overarching development scenario in manners consistent with societal objectives such as economic, racial and social justice. The modern technologies are not constrained by a "bigger is better" mentality, or by other dictates of conventional systems, like the requirement to have a large body of water right close by so your big and massive power plant does not overheat and self-destruct. And third, once the modern technologies are in place and online, the fuel gets delivered to each and every site on a more or less predictable basis, free of extraction and shipping costs, and with no need for negotiations with corporate fuel extractors.

From the 1970s moving forward, the people managing the electric utility industry knew that renewable technologies were slowly getting better and cheaper. As these trends continued and intensified, concerns mounted within the industry that the modern technologies would provide their monopolies with increasingly stiff competition, if it did not just put them out of business. In fact, while monopoly status, complete with properly assigned privileges, is the foundation and the essence of the Central Station Era, the modern renewable energy and energy storage systems invite community-specific capital formations and social structures that are the antithesis of monopoly economics. The question then facing the electric utility industry therefore had to do with how to stop renewable energy resources from being harvested at the utility scale unless and until the industry figured out how the technologies to harvest those resources could be deployed in a manner that protected their market share, and their retail monopoly status.

We know the industry had this concern because we dealt with the fear it generated within the industry on a daily basis throughout the Prairie Island fight over nuclear waste. This struggle began in 1987 and continued through the 1994 Minnesota legislative session, and ultimately produced the wind energy mandates and other provisions that dragged NSP kicking and screaming into the Modern Era. At the very end of the kicking and screaming, after NSP had finally gotten authorization for limited dry cask storage of high-level nuclear waste in exchange for Modern Era energy management and technology provisions, I had a brief conversation with Jim Howard, CEO of NSP at the time. We had several longer ones from time to time, but those are other stories. This brief one was very early in the morning on the very last day of the legislative session, after the Conference Committee and the rest of us had again been up all night, working to block the deal or to get the deal done. Jim approached me as we were down in the big round basement hearing room of the state capitol, both of us exhausted, right after the final vote was taken. "Just so you know, George," he said, "my colleagues are accusing me of giving away the store." What he meant, of course, was that he and his colleagues were afraid, because renewable energy technologies were achieving utility-scale and penetrating electric utility markets before the industry knew how to monopolize them. Then Jim told me he was going to find me a job protecting panthers in the Everglades.

But after NSP's adventure with Zond failed to derail the wind energy mandates, it took NSP only a few years before it got over its bad attitude about renewable energy technologies, and soon it was bragging up its fantastic and stupendously wonderful leadership regarding renewable energy development. "Responsible by nature," it began calling itself, and that's also a story for another time. During those few years, NSP began to understand that the renewable technologies about which it and the rest of the industry had been so fearful, could be mangled and distorted enough to fit into its monopoly playbook quite nicely. NSP, by then Xcel Energy, had figured out the modular nature of the modern technologies. All it had to do was to make renewable energy facilities big enough to mimic central station power plants: large numbers of the largest available wind turbines all clumped together in large, centralized remote wind farms or many tens to hundreds of acres of solar panels, all neatly laid out row upon row, way out somewhere remote. Then, just get the regulators to stick energy consumers with the bill for the high-voltage powerlines required to transmit the power to distant load centers in the cities, and you are good to go. Enthralling concept.

But the rapid change in economies of scale was not the only rapid change occurring in the electric utility industry during the late 1980s and on through the turn of the century. Wholesale electric markets got deregulated during this time, and Independent System Operators (ISOs) were created to manage the competition. Wholesale electric markets were opened up so that anybody with enough money to purchase a utility-scale electric generator could go through the amazingly remarkable process of getting the project hooked up to the grid. Then, the newly interconnected power supplier could either enter bids to sell its power into the wholesale market managed by an ISO, or it could sign a Power Purchase Agreement with a power company to sell all the power it produced to that particular power company, which would then sell the power to its retail customers. Either way, however, before being allowed to connect to the interconnected grid, an electrical generation project needed an Interconnection Agreement issued by the Federal Energy Regulatory Commission (FERC).

As mentioned earlier, the interconnected grid is a truly remarkable engineering achievement. It turns every generation facility hooked up to it into a component of the largest machine ever built. What that means is that at every moment, throughout most of the continent (remembering that the connections between east and west and Texas are less robust), the properly dispatched generation units must produce precisely the amount of electricity that consumers are using at every moment, and powerline voltages and amperages must be maintained precisely as the electricity uniformly pulsates at sixty hertz at every connected location, from the outlet in your wall, to the transformer outside your house, to the distribution lines connecting you to the substations that serve your neighborhood, to the substation transformers connecting distribution lines to the high-voltage system that is connected to generation sources. Precisely. For every end use outlet on the continent. At every instant. Otherwise, circuit breakers trip and ground currents spike and lots of stuff needs fixing.

In other words, managing the interconnected grid is an elaborate balancing act. As with any balancing act, if one were to put a little more weight here, or a little more pressure there, the balance gets disrupted. There was a time, for example, when it was possible, and maybe it still is, to crash parts of the system in Kansas City by overloading a substation in St. Cloud. The amazingly remarkable and painstaking Interconnection Agreement process is required in order to maintain the balance of the interconnected grid, thereby preventing electrical outages. The way it works is that once you know precisely where your new project will be located and exactly what its rated generation capacity is, the extent of the imbalance your project will cause on the interconnected grid can be calculated and proper adjustments can be made. So you tell the FERC how much and where in your application, and then you get to pay a fee that can amount to many tens of thousands of dollars to secure your place in the line of projects waiting for the required analysis. Then you get to wait however many months or whatever, that it takes until it's your turn. The industry calls it "the queue."

When it gets to be your turn, the analysis of your project begins with a power flow model that exactly replicates the electrical environment into which the power from your project will be injected. Then the model adds your contribution, and everybody watches to see what breaks. If you lack unlimited financial resources, you will have selected a project site and size that minimizes the breakage, because you are on the hook for the costs of whatever upgrades the system will require to accommodate the power you will be providing. After installing all the necessary upgrades to transformers and conductors and voltage regulators or whatever, thereby eliminating breakage caused by your project, you are good to go if you have a Power Purchase Agreement with a purchasing power company. If you are an Independent Power Producer, you will be in business whenever the market reaches your bid price.

But now, after you got your project connected, it's a different interconnected transmission system because of your contribution and all the enhancements that were made to accommodate your project, which means that it will be this new, enhanced system that will be modeled for the project next in line after you. This iterative process, one project at a time, is what enables the big machine to work, but causes projects to wait in the queue for considerable periods of time. This waiting has led those who can afford it to game the system by submitting applications for proxy projects, placeholders, if you will. When a proxy project comes up for analysis, a well-heeled developer who has multiple projects in the queue could substitute a project deeper in the queue, but with better prospects for analysis. This works fine for large institutional players, but it places smaller projects that lack deep pockets and may be more connected to specific communities at a competitive disadvantage. Regardless of the interconnection process, however, when large, corporate power producers channel the development of renewable energy facilities into formations that mimic an obsolete, central station monopoly paradigm, the industry ends up managing the overall transmission system upside down, which we will discuss shortly.

A third factor has to do with the nature of institutional change: what is required to transition from one set of major societal circumstances to another. As the electric utility paradigm began shifting, differences between public interests and power company interests became increasingly apparent. Voices representing public interests became increasingly involved with electric utility decision-making proceedings in order to represent interests at odds with what the electric utility industry wanted to do, interests that were not adequately represented by the regulating bureaucracy. Some of these voices were motivated by issues raised, for example, by dubious application of eminent domain procedures. Others were more intent on catalyzing the transformation of the industry, with the objective of guiding it and its regulators toward delivering cleaner and more equitable energy services.

From the beginning of the electric utility industry on through the 1960s and into the 1970s, there was little if any formal intervention by third parties in electric utility decision-making proceedings, mainly because there were few, if any proceedings regarding how electric utility infrastructure would be developed. Power companies built what they wanted to build, or purchased smaller fish, so to speak, and pollution was hardly a topic of discussion. The attention of regulators was pretty much focused on how much power companies could charge for their services, which was not much of an issue either, seeing as how central station economies of scale were in full force and effect, making electricity penny cheap to you.

That all started changing as the Arab Oil Embargo of 1973 forced polite society, such as it is, to begin considering energy resources as valuable commodities that needed to be managed properly instead of merely substances that got extracted and consumed. Laws got passed. Rules were promulgated. Bureaucracies, like Minnesota's Pollution Control Agency and the Environmental Quality Board and the Department of Public Service emerged. But still, through the 1970s and into the 1980s, while the bureaucracies participated in electric utility decision-making proceedings, the public, largely, did not. The Senior Federation intervened in certain rate cases, but that was about it.

Then the paradigm began shifting in earnest because wind and solar technologies kept improving, so the divergence of interests kept becoming more apparent and dramatic. Regulators now had much more to do than just argue over rates, but they are still regulators, not change agents. This was the breach into which I jumped, first with the powerline fight, then TKO, and continuing on as the North American Water Office intervened strategically in docket after docket, helping to direct the early beginnings of the ongoing campaign for a CLEAR energy future.

High-voltage transmission planning and development also evolved during the Central Station Era. In its early days, each utility jurisdiction maintained enough electrical generation capacity to meet its native load all the time, except maybe during emergency situations. The primary function performed by high-voltage transmission in these earlier days was therefore to enhance reliability. The high-voltage grid enabled neighboring and regional electric utility jurisdictions to support each other during times of stress due to weather and technical difficulties. If, for some reason, an electric utility was experiencing a power or delivery capability shortage within its system, the high-voltage interconnected grid made it possible to fill gaps by replacing and re-routing power flows.

This primary function of the grid changed dramatically when competition entered electric utility wholesale markets beginning in the late 1980s and early 1990s. While the grid retained its reliability functions, after deregulation, wholesale power marketers were able to use the interconnected grid to deliver power to loads from generation capacity that was dispatched *economically*, as opposed to generation that was attached to specific power company service territories. The order in which electrical generation comes online was no longer determined by the power company managing its own internal loads within its service territory, but instead through the ISO bidding process whereby the cheapest power in the pool of bid capacity gets brought online first regardless of ownership, and the dispatch order follows the daily load duration curve throughout the day with the most expensive bid power shut off first as loads decrease in the evening and on into the night.

If power companies want to sell power that they produce from power plants that they own and that were originally built to serve customers within their service territory, after wholesale competition got introduced, they were required to bid the generation capacity that they owned into the ISO pools, along with all the other wholesale power supply competitors. If they want their power plants to generate electricity, they need to bid the prices at which they are willing to sell at prices that compete favorably with all the other wholesale market participants.

An unfortunate reality that accompanies wholesale competition in electric utility markets is that the market competition is rigged. In order for markets, any markets, including electric utility markets, to be free and fair, the full cost of the product being sold must be included in the price paid for it, with maybe a sale from time to time. In many markets, there is ongoing discussion, with varying degrees of sophistication and decorum, about what is or isn't, or should or should not be included in the full and fair cost of the product being sold. The electric utility industry is different. It does not count anything approaching the actual cost of the damage being done by Greenhouse gasses, or the cost of damage done by acid gasses or toxic metals, or the cost of liability insurance for nuclear reactors, or the cost of managing irradiated nuclear fuel for 240,000 years, or the actual value as opposed to the market price of extracted energy resources, or externalized extraction costs that sometimes includes warring, and so forth. There's a whole list of "externalities." So it is not surprising that the electric utility industry, including wholesale competitors, is able to manage its regulatory affairs so that it also does not have to pay transmission costs attached to its projects that are above and beyond interconnection enhancements required to hook up to the existing grid.

This externalization of transmission costs is among the factors that provide a competitive advantage to large capital formations developing, owning and profiting from remote renewable energy projects the size of central station power plants, as opposed to energy development that recognizes the overall welfare of each community that receives electric utility services. Another factor that prevents free and fair competition in competitive wholesale electric utility markets are laws like Minnesota Statute 216B.45 that are designed specifically to *prevent* such competition. As mentioned earlier, if a city wants cleaner energy than the power company is selling, or wants to rein in electricity rates within its jurisdiction by municipalizing the electric utility infrastructure that serves its residents, this law requires it to not only purchase that infrastructure from the incumbent utility, but to also pay that incumbent utility the profits that it would make absent the purchase of the infrastructure. As far as power companies are concerned, this is a "heads I win, tails you lose" situation.

Competition in wholesale electric markets gets directed even further away from economic democracy and toward increasing concentrations of capital by the fact that virtually all utility-scale renewable energy projects in the US depend on passive income production tax credits from the federal government. Wealthy people and institutions have passive income. Most of us do not. Passive income is not earned with the sweat of your brow or by any of your other talents, whatever they may be. Passive income is money you get from stock sales and dividends, from rental income, interest payments and other revenue streams that flow from accumulated wealth. Passive income is taxed at rates of up to twenty percent, depending on your taxable income.

For wealthy individuals and institutions, these tax rates can amount to tens, or even hundreds of millions of dollars of tax liability, which is where passive income tax credits come into play.

Passive income production tax credits create opportunities for individuals and institutions with passive income tax liabilities to invest their taxable passive income into projects and programs that qualify for production tax credits. Then, the amount of money they owe in passive income taxes will become an investment that will earn them a return, instead of costing them the money that would otherwise go into the coffers of the federal government. Passive income production tax credits therefore provide an extremely effective tool for incentivizing desired behavior, such as wind turbines, for example, and passive income tax credits have driven the vast majority of all the utility-scale renewable energy investments made in the United States. But they are also remarkably efficient at concentrating wealth in the hands of just the few. Over time, this amounts to hundreds of billions of dollars of unearned wealth getting transferred from electric utility ratepayers to extremely wealthy power producers. Maybe you can think of other terms for "unearned transfer of wealth."

Anyway, by the time, shortly after the turn of the century, that it became apparent that the electric utility paradigm shift was irreversible, the number of non-governmental renewable energy advocates actively engaged with interventions in regulated electric utility decision-making proceedings in Minnesota had proliferated into a dozen or more organizations that recognized the need to define and defend public interests as the electric utility industry was getting itself adjusted. Concern about Climate Chaos was increasing, and we all understood that in order to make much difference from an environmental perspective, an awful lot of renewable energy needed to get developed and come online quickly.

But only a relatively few of us understood that such a transformation was unlikely to happen in time, so long as the unearned transfer of wealth continued. Unless that profound flaw was corrected, we reasoned, the vast majority of people who pay an electric bill and just expect the light to come on when they flip the switch, would remain indifferent to the energy transition. Without their informed and active involvement, at least in terms of supporting a political agenda, we did not think there was much of a chance of getting enough renewable energy online or getting it in time. Even worse, we feared the "pig shit principle." We were quite certain that if people in communities affected by renewable energy projects had a direct economic stake in those projects through ownership of them, the projects in which they participated would smell a lot like money. Otherwise, we worried that communities affected by massive, central station-like renewable energy developments would become not just indifferent, but actively opposed to wind and solar projects. For them, the disruptions, and perhaps the cost of improving roads during construction, or the flicker and noise of spinning turbine blades, or land use issues, along with the ongoing extraction of wealth from their communities would cause renewable energy to just stink. We wanted to promote public support for renewable energy and minimize public opposition.

Meanwhile, the more mainstream advocacy organizations claimed to be agnostic regarding who owned the means of production in the burgeoning renewable energy economy. They recognized the environmental imperative of getting lots of renewable electric generation capacity online quickly, and acted on the notion that the deep pockets of the electric utility industry would make that happen if only they were ordered to do so. No sooner had the paradigm shifted, therefore, than a split developed among us non-governmental renewable energy advocates. The split was over two closely related issues: which renewable energy development scenarios best served public interests, and who should participate in the ownership structures of the renewable energy projects that were rapidly penetrating electric utility markets.

For our part, we wanted to take advantage of the versatility renewable technologies offer and turn the imperative to clean up the environment into an economic development opportunity that would be available to people in virtually every community in the state. Our team formed around the same wind developer who testified on our behalf during the Prairie Island nuclear waste hearings, and who got abused by NSP during the bidding process for the mandated wind. We went for C-BED: Community-Based Energy Development, while the mainstream organizations went for legislation that would establish Renewable Energy Standards (RES).

By 2005, with utility-scale renewable energy clearly here to stay, the question was therefore how to bring it forward. Republicans controlled the House of Representatives and held the Governor's seat at that time, with the Democratic Farmer Labor (DFL) Party having the majority in the Senate. The Republicans hated RES and were still not all that keen on renewables but knew that things were changing, while the DFL loved renewables but lacked the votes to do much about it. Petty politics also got in the way, as southwestern Minnesota, along the Buffalo Ridge, has one of the world's richest wind resources, but it's also farm country dominated by relatively well-to-do Republican farmers, which was reason enough for a fair amount of opposition from some of the "Ds." When we brought our C-BED proposal to the Governor's staff, therefore, they loved it, and while there was some genuine Republican enthusiasm for it, there were also substantial forces at play that were more interested in using C-BED as a foil against RES. We organized and influenced well enough so that the Minnesota Legislature passed C-BED legislation in 2005, a couple years before the mainstream groups got their RES in 2007.

While we celebrated with a joyous ceremony in the Capitol as the Governor signed our C-BED legislation into law in 2005, C-BED never really caught on for any number of reasons, some more obvious than others. An early clue was that, as we were crafting the legislation, the politicians told those of us aiming for economic democracy that we had to negotiate the bill's actual language with electric utility lawyers and lobbyists. In other words, power companies, who had the most powerful lobby force at the Capitol, and who had the most to lose should C-BED be successful, were given a veto over any provision in the C-BED statute that they did not like. If we wanted any form of C-BED, we were required to agree with terms and conditions in the C-BED legislation that met the approval of the Minnesota power companies that would purchase C-BED power. One of the major consequences of this struggle over the language in the C-BED legislation, therefore, was that while it created a requirement for regulated power companies to enter into *negotiations* with qualifying C-BED projects, there was no requirement for power companies to *actually sign* any Power Purchase Agreements with C-BED projects. The situation was further complicated by the fact that whatever we did, it would only apply in Minnesota even though transmission lines do not care much about state boundaries, and we also needed to keep from running afoul of federal Interstate Commerce Clauses.

Nonetheless, we did our best, with limited success, to establish a C-BED process that would encourage people in their own communities to get financially organized enough to attract somewhere between $5 and $50 million for their very own utility-scale wind farm. Well, not quite their own, due to the need for passive income tax credits, but if we were successful, the process would lead to the formation of projects that were sized to meet the needs of communities in which they were located, with locally owned Limited Liability Corporations (LLC) included in the ownership structure, and through a Power Purchase Agreement, sell their power to a Minnesota-based power company while circulating energy dollars locally.

Our understanding of the difficulties facing C-BED continued to improve as we learned more about the complicated and expensive transmission interconnection process that C-BED projects were required to navigate. How many people do you know who have many thousands of dollars sitting around that they can afford to spend on getting in a line to wait for a large but unspecified number of months while monied interests find ways to keep jumping in front of you? Even more daunting were the issues created by the overwhelming role passive income plays in creating the capital formations that create renewable energy projects. Passive income production tax credits amount to free money from the federal government for those wealthy enough to have access to them, and because it is not possible to out-compete free money, it is necessary to attract it if you want to have a project that can participate in wholesale electric markets. The financial gymnastics required to do so are spectacular, and Dan, our wind developer friend from the early 1990s, figured it out by creating "the Minnesota Flip." You can go online and get the details if you want. Needless to say, with all these obstacles stunting C-BED development, there are relatively few C-BED projects selling power to purchasing utilities.

Meanwhile, the mainstream groups got their RES in 2007. While renewable energy standards have been met, they tend to be more ceiling than floor, and electric utility managers continue to wring every last nickel out of their central station machines while the pace of our collective march deeper into Climate Chaos continues to accelerate.

So, our situation is that C-BED got more or less thwarted, and renewable energy standards, obviously, are not succeeding if environmental protection is the objective. C-BED and RES are circumstances with which I am familiar, and most certainly others in other jurisdictions around the country and around the world are dealing with their own circumstances, and continue trying to reverse, or at least decelerate the impacts of Climate Chaos. Whatever it is that "all we of us" are doing, though, isn't enough. Something more is needed, which is where the upside-down part comes in. While C-BED was not a success in terms of bringing significant amounts of renewable energy online, pursuing C-BED projects enabled us to learn that a big part of this upside down something has to do with dramatically shifting the way in which the interconnected grid gets managed.

Throughout the Central Station Era, the fundamental reality has been that power *always* flows from the top down. Power *always* flowed from big remote generators through a series of transformers and conductors until it reached its end-use. But now with C-BED, for the first time ever, utility managers, especially transmission engineers, had to think about how a large number of relatively small electric generators, dispersed and distributed throughout a region could get connected to their interconnected grid.

For our part, once we got C-BED legislation passed, our efforts were directed toward developing C-BED projects. This required public education to help people in their own communities understand the opportunity and get organized to take advantage of it, and it also required identifying potential sites for C-BED projects. Understanding how the interconnected grid is structured and managed was a big part of this work, considering that a substation connecting a project with a 345 kV line could cost upward of $10 million, while the cost of connecting to a sixty-nine kV line could be under $1 million. Cash-flow only goes so far, and $10 million of added cost for a substation is out of reach for most C-BED projects.

A project strategically sized for a specific site according to available transmission infrastructure might not clear the interconnection queue any quicker, but it could certainly make the interconnection process cheaper. We started studying transmission maps and familiarizing ourselves with Minnesota's six transmission territories, and learning about power flow models, and we introduced ourselves to the happy band of transmission engineers employed by Minnesota's power companies.

As a result, in the Autumn of 2005, the North American Water Office negotiated with a utility consortium to set the terms and conditions of The Community-Based Energy Development Transmission Study that focused on how allowing interconnection to the transmission system on lower voltage transmission lines could enable local ownership of C-BED projects. The study examined the seventeen county area of the West Central Minnesota Transmission Planning Zone, encompassing more than 540,000 people and nearly 11,300 square miles. This power flow analysis examined transmission enhancement costs of adding new dispersed generation on the high-voltage side of all fifty-seven substations in that region operating at 115 kV or less.

The results of this study caused a bit of excitement among the transmission engineering community, bearing in mind that the *total* electric load in the West Central Minnesota Transmission Planning Zone is less than a couple thousand megawatts. The results showed that 800 MW of new dispersed generation could be installed at these fifty-seven sites *without requiring any new transmission.* A second increment of 200 MW could be installed if a new 115 kV line costing $10 - $15 million were constructed. A third increment of 400 MW could be installed with an upgrade to a phase-shifting transformer costing about $25 million up by International Falls, of which we'll hear more about shortly. In total, this analysis identified 3,500 MW of new electrical generation capacity that could be installed in the West Central region at a cost for new transmission infrastructure of about $60,000 per megawatt of generation capacity, compared to new transmission costs of over $900,000 per megawatt of new generation capacity for remote, concentrated wind or solar farm developments. When the transmission engineers applied the same analytical methodology and parameters to all five of the non-urban Minnesota Transmission Planning zones (all Minnesota except for the Twin Cities), they found that for the same transmission upgrade cost of about $60,000 per installed megawatt, 13,752 megawatts of new distributed and dispersed generation capacity could be installed strategically around the state. For perspective, in 2005 Minnesota had a total of about 12,000 MW of electrical generation capacity.

The remarkable results from the West Central Minnesota Transmission Study, along with our community education and organizing efforts, created the leverage that the North American Water Office and our C-BED partners needed to make the case for a deeper, state-wide study of the transmission system's ability to accommodate strategically sized distributed and dispersed generation. The politicians agreed and directed us to negotiate the parameters of a more comprehensive analysis with our new transmission engineer friends, which we did. As a result, the Minnesota Legislature passed a law that established the

2008 Dispersed Renewable Generation Study. The idea was to understand the cost of new transmission infrastructure required to optimize deployment of distributed and dispersed generation but imagine our surprise when we discovered that the power flow model to conduct such an analysis did not exist.

Up until that moment, each individual power company maintained power flow models of its entire system, including and integrating both high-voltage transmission components and distribution components. And collectively, all the power companies together maintained power flow models of the state-wide and regional high-voltage transmission system that connected them all together and that they all used when making decisions about high-voltage transmission system enhancements. In the Central Station Era, that was all they needed. There was no use for a power flow model that integrated the entire interconnected system because in the Central Station Era, power *always* flowed from the top down. Because there was no meaningful development of dispersed and distributed generation, there was no need to understand the generation outlet capacity of the transmission system. It was simply not possible for any enhancements or additions to lower voltage transmission systems, or distribution systems, to have any impact at all on the high-voltage transmission system. Power just did not flow that way. That changed when the dispersed and distributed renewable energy technologies of the Modern Era started to get deployed.

To understand the emerging system, we successfully lobbied and convinced pertinent politicians, we now needed a fully integrated power flow model of the entire state. But the happy band of transmission engineers was not pleased. It was a tedious process, it took them months, and they whined about it the entire time because in order to model a fully integrated high-and-low voltage system, they had to physically inject their presence into their power flow modeling and manually connect each and every lower voltage distribution substation connection point properly to the higher voltage model of their system. It's not like power flowing in the distribution system was ignored during Central Station Era power flow modeling, it's just that it was not relevant to Central Station Era transmission planning. All they had to do back then was arbitrarily lump distribution voltage power flows together and then inject their lump into the high-voltage transmission power flow model somewhere, almost anywhere, and they were good to go. When the Minnesota Legislature required the 2008 Dispersed Renewable Generation Transmission Study to be conducted, those days were over.

Unfortunately, even as politicians and bureaucrats realized the need for this brand new fully integrated power flow model, we fell victim to the same political trap that effectively neutered C-BED. The politicians, in their wisdom, required those of us seeking a semblance of economic democracy for renewable energy development to again negotiate the terms and specific conditions of the 2008 Dispersed Renewable Generation Transmission Study with the parties that had the most to lose, should we successfully document the potential to saturate the existing interconnected transmission system with thousands of megawatts of strategically sized and located generation. So once again, we did our best to hold our own against a small army of electric utility lawyers, lobbyists, and this time also utility transmission engineers. They teamed up with the "expert" hired by the bureaucrats to oversee the negotiations.

From our perspective, the negotiations did not go well. For example, the size of projects to be included in the study was important for the obvious reason that a larger number of smaller objects can fit into a given space, and we wanted lots and lots of objects. But if the objects are bigger, fewer will fit. And strategically placed, the smaller sizes can fill up more of the given space. We therefore wanted the size of projects in the study to be from two MW, which is about as small as utility-scale projects get, up to forty MW because community-based projects are not likely to get much bigger. But no. The utilities and their expert decided the lower limit would be ten MW, so the results were skewed toward the old paradigm from the start.

The study was to be conducted in two phases. Phase 1 would determine how much additional generation capacity between ten MW and forty MW the *existing* fully integrated high-and-low voltage state-wide interconnected grid (except for the Twin Cities) could accept. Being as we were the ones who brought the study idea forward, and who were charged by the politicians with negotiating its terms, Mike, my electrical engineer partner and I were included on the team that designed the study. Then they went and ran the model without including a critical component, the aforementioned phase-shifting transformer up by International Falls needed to manage imports from Manitoba Hydro. This transformer had been identified as a critical component for years, ever since Manitoba Hydro began to export power to the states, but the industry was still arguing over who should pay the $25 million it would cost. Including it in the model would have way more than doubled the amount of new generation outlet capacity that Phase 1 would have reported that the system could accommodate.

The decision to not include this phase-shifting transformer in the Phase 1 analysis was caused by the same fear that made NSP fight so hard, for so many years, over nuclear waste at Prairie Island. Including it in the study would enable large amounts of renewable generation capacity to come online before the power companies had figured out how it could be deployed in ways that protected their market share and their monopoly. Not including it was a deliberate ploy to sabotage the study results. We argued for weeks over this profound failure. When the futility of our argument was apparent, because the self-serving bureaucrats and electric utility transmission engineers would not even include a footnote about the impact this one transformer would have, we went public with our concern. Then the bureaucrats and their expert hired help got angry with us and kicked us off the study management team.

Phase 2 was therefore conducted without us. The bureaucrats and engineers ran their model after adding certain transmission enhancements already under consideration and that were illuminated by

Phase 1, including the phase-shifting transformer up by International Falls. Unfortunately, without us instigators to keep the industry and its bureaucrats honest, they added their transmission enhancements all right, but then they also added to the model every single megawatt that was signed up in the queue prior to running the model, which amounted to thousands of megawatts. The thing about the queue that we have discussed is that it's a long, expensive, arduous process to get your project interconnected. Another thing about the queue that we have not discussed is that less than half the projects in it ever make it to an actual Interconnection Agreement.

Yet, these reasonably intelligent engineers and lawyers and bureaucrats injected the full amount of electrical generation capacity waiting in line for a grid interconnection study, into their fully integrated high-and-low voltage transmission power flow model. They injected it into the model prior to running it to find out how much dispersed and distributed electrical generation capacity the enhanced grid could accommodate. In other words, they crammed thousands of megawatts of imaginary generation capacity into their model, and every one of these imaginary megawatts displaced a megawatt of the dispersed and distributed generation that the study was designed and intended to discover. Lo and behold, modeled results showed that the reinforced, interconnected Minnesota grid could not even accept 100 MW of new distributed and dispersed generation.

Then the bureaucrats and power company lawyers and engineers presented their findings to legislative committees on which not one of the politicians was informed enough to know that they were being snookered, or smart enough to ask an intelligent question. Then the bureaucrats and power company lawyers and engineers lied further by testifying to the legislative committees that the model went all the way down to 5 MW, and that even then, it could not identify a significant additional opportunity to use the interconnected grid more efficiently.

Having been banished for crying "FOUL" during Phase 1, Mike and I had been effectively removed from the discussion. We had no say regarding methodology or conclusions that the bureaucrats, utility lawyers and engineers presented to the politicians. As they made their presentation, an outrage and utter disgust welled up within me at those cheating, lying, thieving, murderously despicable two-leggeds who were perpetrating this heinous fraud, and it overwhelmed me. I could leave or get busted maybe for aggravated assault or perhaps something in the third degree. I left. I never went back. But then, it turned out that I did not need to, and how all that unfolded will be examined shortly.

For now, suffice it to say that renewable energy advocates in California were paying attention to our Dispersed Renewable Generation Transmission Study. They replicated our methodology but did so honestly. Somewhere around 2013, I found out that we had been vindicated by their results. Their replication, adapted for California circumstances, revealed that the existing California grid could accommodate strategically sized and located dispersed and distributed generation amounting to over thirty percent of California's installed generation capacity, which amounted to something over 20,000 megawatts of new generation.

With this as a benchmark, and recognizing both the differences between Minnesota and California in terms of geography and population distribution, as well as the results of the 2005 West Central Minnesota C-BED Study, it is reasonable to postulate that had Minnesota done an honest job of it, the Phase 2 analysis would have documented an opportunity to add something more than forty percent of Minnesota's installed generation capacity to the existing grid without the need for *any* new high-voltage transmission lines. That would amount to something north of 5,000 MW of new electric generation capacity that could get installed within the existing system.

5,000 MW of new electric generation could have been developed and brought online with next to nothing in terms of new transmission infrastructure costs. All of this new generation capacity would have been developed near the communities served by the new capacity, with profound implications for the advent of economic democracy.

What did we get instead? We got CAPX-2020, the electric utility industry's idea of a good time, actively supported by Minnesota's bureaucrats and politicians and proponents of RES. CAPX 2020 was the reason behind the lying, cheating thievery in both phases of Minnesota's integrated transmission analysis. CAPX 2020 consists of about 600 miles of new 345 kV transmission, at a cost of about $2.1 billion, and that provides transmission outlet capacity for about 1,900 megawatts of new, remote electric generating capacity.

As a society, we had a choice. On one hand, we could have chosen around 5,000 MW of new generation capacity with little or no new transmission costs, the development of which would promote economic democracy. On the other, we had 1,900 MW of new generation owned by and enriching outside interests well-endowed with passive income and requiring the consuming public to pay for new transmission costing $2,100,000,000.00. In our collective wisdom, which option do you think we chose?

Despite the glaringly stupid ignorance and corruption that allows such ignominious decisions to be made routinely and repeatedly throughout the country, opportunities to deliver the supply side of electric utility services properly still remain before our collective selves. Grid management can be reimagined to take full advantage of the modular versatility in size and siting provided by renewable energy and energy storage technologies. This modularity means renewable energy projects can be deployed with specific sizes that fit specific electrical requirements at specific interconnection sites. This allows us to begin the process of transforming the interconnected grid from the bottom up, and this transformation can occur at a suitable site reasonably close to any substation, whether the substation is out in the country, in the suburbs or in a city. All you need is a substation that serves a retail load. Such substations are typically connected to the higher voltage system with transformers that step the voltage down to anywhere between thirty-four and a half kV to somewhere around three or four kV, depending on the loads a particular substation is serving.

For example, let's say that we have a hypothetical substation that connects a 115 kV high-voltage powerline with a distribution line that serves the electrical load within the footprint of the substation, and the distribution line operates at 13.5 kV. The load served within that footprint has its own miniature load duration curve, with daily highs and lows that follow seasonal patterns. Let's presume, hypothetically, that the annual maximum load within this substation footprint is ten megawatts, and the minimum annual load is four megawatts, which would occur in the springtime or autumn at night when everyone's asleep and the weather's nice so neither space heating or cooling is needed. This is where the versatility of modular renewable technologies comes into play.

If electrical generation capacity is connected to the low voltage side of the 115 kV/13.5 kV transformer, and the electric generator has a rated capacity less than the minimum annual load within the footprint of the substation, *all* the power produced by the generator will be consumed within the substation footprint, and *no* power will ever get pushed back up into the higher voltage system. All the power generated by such a generator will be consumed within the footprint of the substation, and every bit of it will back out electricity that would otherwise get generated by a remote central station facility. In other words, considering that the minimum annual load within our hypothetical footprint is four megawatts, if the renewable energy generator is rated at 3.5 megawatts, the overall system has just installed 3.5 new megawatts without the need for any new transmission infrastructure.

This renewable energy development scenario can be applied to *every* substation on the interconnected grid that serves a retail load, throughout North America. This means that many tens of thousands of new megawatts of clean, renewable energy could be online within a year, or as fast as the modular units of generation can be manufactured and installed, with virtually all of it displacing fossil and nuclear generating capacity, thereby mitigating against the ravages of Climate Chaos and the myriad of nasty issues attached to nuclear power.

The next step in getting a properly managed electric utility system would be to strategically deploy generation capacity that would be connected to the high-voltage side of qualifying substations, which would be almost all of them. The deployment strategy would be guided by results from power flow modeling, such as was sabotaged during our Phase 1 and Phase 2 transmission study adventures. This renewable energy development strategy is made possible by the fact that electrical transformers do not care which way the power flows. Electricity simply follows the path of least resistance. Power flows through transformers from lower to higher voltages just as easily as it flows the other way around. Central station generation inherently caused power to flow through the interconnected grid from higher voltages to lower voltages as it got transmitted to points of end use, but the direction of the power flow makes no difference to transformers. In other words, when we get energy right, power flow on the interconnected grid will not be unidirectional. Rather, it will depend on which dispersed and distributed renewable generation and energy storage facilities are online at any point in time, which ones are not, where they are located relative to all the other sources of online generation, and what the electrical loading is at all relevant points of end use.

The deployment of the first iteration of this dispersed and distributed electric generation capacity would, in turn, inform decision-making about how to strategically enhance the lower end of the higher voltage system to accommodate the next increment of dispersed and distributed renewable energy projects. Then we would do another power flow analysis to determine the next increment of transmission enhancements. Within a few short years, this iterative process would enable the deployment of enough dispersed and distributed renewable energy and storage capacity to allow all central station power plants to be retired, with the possible exception of a few big power plants to serve the densest of industrial loads. As this development strategy unfolds, there would be no need for any new power lines on the higher end of the voltage spectrum.

This electric utility development strategy recognizes the fact that wind and solar energy resources can be cost-effectively harvested even in regions that do not have the world's richest wind and solar regimes. There are a number of regions on our planet that have very high average annual wind speeds, and there are parts of Earth where the solar resource is of a higher value than others. But detailed studies of wind patterns that have been conducted over decades document thousands upon thousands of locations where harvestable winds blow hard enough to warrant very cost-effective wind projects. Likewise with the sun. Locations with very economically harvestable solar resources are abundant. And as stated earlier, when transmission costs are included in the cost of developing large, remote wind and solar projects, the dispersed and distributed development strategy is in all instances very competitive, and usually much more cost-effective.

Among the numerous and major advantages of this dispersed and distributed electric generation development strategy is that it creates an electric utility system that is much more resilient and robust than a system dominated by a relatively few big central station power plants. This resiliency stems from the same reason that trees do not have just a few very big leaves. *Brittle Power*, published by Amory Lovins and the Rocky Mountain Institute in 1982 was an early warning of vulnerabilities inherent to central station development, and that vulnerability only increases as the volatility of political and climactic circumstances increases.

Much of this vulnerability disappears with a distributed and dispersed electric system, however, because most of the big targets that would cause major disruptions if they were eliminated have been replaced with a very large number of generators scattered about, making targeting difficult. The dispersed and distributed pattern of deployment is also a good starting point for "smart" microgrids, whereby relatively small groupings of local homes and smaller businesses are hooked together, with at least part of the electrical generation capacity they require internalized within their microgrid circuit. Each microgrid is then connected electrically with each of its neighboring microgrids. A community saturated with microgrids is less vulnerable to massive power outages caused by Climate Chaos's increasingly severe storms that are becoming a daily staple on the nightly network news, because more electrical generation capacity is available locally, and repairing local distribution lines is quicker, easier and cheaper than repairing higher voltage transmission lines required by remote central station generators.

Then, there are the equity issues. Economic democracy. When the electrical system is developed in a dispersed and distributed manner, it becomes easier for people in their own communities to understand and to become involved with the systems that provide them with electric utility services. With this understanding and involvement comes an ability to establish public policy that encourages capital formations that generate wealth, not for outside interests with an appetite for passive income tax credits, but for local community interests that benefit from the circulation of energy dollars created by kilowatt hours that are produced and consumed locally. The local economy is further enhanced by the creation of numerous good-paying jobs that become available to community members. The local tax-base is expanded, creating new opportunities for any number of educational, public health and other civic-minded programs. There is no end to the positive societal results that we will be able to enjoy when we get energy right.

# Chapter 6

## NUKES

The thing about commercial nuclear power is that it cannot pay its own freight. It never could and never has, right from the very beginning. Actually, there's quite a list of things about commercial nuclear power that ought to disqualify it as an option for participating in electric utility markets, and we'll examine a few of them. But in a free market economy, such as we purport to have in these United States, not being able to pay the expenses that you incur in the course of your participation in commercial markets is basic, fundamental failure. It is disqualifying, and rightly so. Except for the commercial nuclear industry, it's not. For the commercial nuclear industry, this failure has persisted since the 1950s, and it has not mattered. The massive subsidies continue. If you think that market forces should be guiding electric utility markets, knowing a bit about why the commercial nuclear industry is able to circumvent fundamental principles of a free-market economy will make it easier to understand why the expeditious phase-out of commercial nuclear power should be completed with expedition.

In fairness, the electric utility industry never asked for nuclear power. But the Cold War was raging, and it would be easier to win the nuclear arms race against Godless Communists, reasoned our Cold Warriors, if there were a civilian side to the nuclear industry. "Atoms for Peace," they called it, with promises of electricity "too cheap to me-ter." Under this banner, the federal government developed the technology for both fission technologies online today, boiling water and pressurized water reactors. They are reactors in which uranium atoms get smashed and explode in chain reactions that produce prodigious amounts of heat. All the many billions of dollars' worth of research and development required to bring these technologies into the commercial energy arena was provided by federal government money. When our Cold Warriors were confident enough that their publicly funded nuclear technologies were mature enough for commercialization, they presented them like a gift to the electric utility industry.

In boiling water reactors, primary water from a nearby river, large lake or ocean gets properly treated and then pumped into the reactor core where it comes in direct contact with fuel assemblies and flashes to steam. The steam gets channeled and directed to keep a turbine spinning so that the generator generates. After leaving the turbine, the spent steam phase-shifts back to water in a condenser, where it gets pumped back to the reactor core for reheating. Secondary water from the nearby river, large lake or ocean gets pumped through the condenser, where it absorbs residual heat from the primary loop and is then released back into the large body of water. We will get into details regarding pressurized water reactors in a bit. For now, these are the two types of reactors that our Cold Warriors provided to the industry in this country, but there are other reactor designs. Cold Warriors on the other side of the Iron Curtain developed a graphite-moderated reactor core that may have come to your attention in a movie about Chernobyl. And for quite a while in this country, there was enthusiasm for a sodium-cooled "breeder" reactor, but that did not work out due to a partial core meltdown in 1966 during which we almost lost Detroit. Brian Jackson and Gill Scott Heron wrote a song about it. More on that also, shortly.

All told, there are ninety-four commercially operating nuclear reactors in the United States. Sixty-three of them are pressurized water reactors, and thirty-one are boiling water reactors. The importance of every one of them having access to large bodies of water cannot be overemphasized. As Climate Chaos increasingly works its will across the Earth's surface, the associated floods and droughts will impact the availability of cooling water for many reactors. These circumstances will prevent rivers, in particular, from providing the absolutely essential cooling water required for both nuclear and coal plants, but if it's a coal plant, it can just shut down until water becomes available again. Not so with reactors. If there is irradiated fuel in a reactor's core or in its spent fuel storage pool, lack of cooling water will in due course result in catastrophic radioactive releases to the environment. As Climate Chaos intensifies and water availability becomes increasingly dubious, the reliability of commercial reactors, as well as all the other thermal plants that require water to boil into steam to spin turbines, will diminish.

In any event, the US electric utility industry was unimpressed by the wondrous gift offered by our Cold Warriors. The big coal-fired power plants owned and operated by power companies were still getting ever bigger, so electricity was getting ever cheaper to produce, and all the soot was barely noticed, and nobody knew or cared about the mercury and the suite of other toxic metals getting smelted out of the big coal fires and released to the environment for biological consumption, and acid rain and Climate Chaos were decades away from even being part of anyone's perception of reality. Who needed a whole new and extraordinarily complicated, dangerous way to boil water? Well, the Cold Warriors did, and in those days, Cold Warriors got what they wanted because it was their job to keep the Red Menace in check no matter what.

Not having paid for any of the costs to design commercial nuclear technologies, or for developing commercial nuclear power operational controls and infrastructure, power companies had no clue as to how to go about running nuclear power plants. "No problem," said the Cold Warriors. "Not only will we give you the technology, but we'll also provide you with all the nuclear engineers and technicians you need to build and operate the plants." And they did. Power companies still balked, and were adamant regarding liability concerns, because they realized that an untoward incident at a commercial nuclear reactor could not only wipe out the power company, but also the power company's entire service territory. Maybe a number of neighboring service territories, as well. "No problem," said the Cold Warriors, "We'll indemnify you against anything that could possibly go wrong at virtually no cost to you." And they did. It's called the Price-Anderson Act, and in 1957, it amended Sec. 170 of the Atomic Energy Act of 1954 (42 USC 2210), which has been extended and amended many times since. These days, in a very convoluted and opaque manner, it continues to shield power companies from virtually all damages in the event of a catastrophic occurrence at their nuclear reactors, and Price-Anderson essentially caps the federal government's liability per event at somewhere around $700 million, which these days, is a relatively low price for an entire power company service territory or three or maybe five or six. In such an event, very large amounts of deadly radioactive material would be dispersed over a very large area.

The financial shields and caps provided by Price-Anderson are essential for commercial nuclear operations because of radiation. Some nuclear materials are extremely radioactive and can kill most living things quickly and continue doing so for extremely long periods of time. Plutonium, for example, is an unavoidable part of the nuclear fuel chain. Plutonium has a half-life of 24,000 years, the time it takes for half of its radioactivity to decay and dissipate. The "rule of thumb" is that radioactive substances need to pass through ten half-lives before they are relatively benign, biologically speaking. Such extended management time-periods and the certainty of massive damages caused by unprogrammed radiation releases would make nuclear power impossible without Price-Anderson indemnification.

Then there's the hundreds of thousands of metric tons of low and high-level nuclear waste produced by nuclear power plants, but that power companies had not even a foggy idea as to how to manage for the required period of time, and it is unlikely that they even knew what the required period of time is. "No problem," said the Cold Warriors, even though they knew no more than the power companies about the specifications of proper nuclear waste management programs. "We'll be the ones," they said, "not you, who are ultimately responsible for all the waste." To this very day, neither the United States, nor any other country on Earth is much closer to figuring out how to safely bequeath these radioactive materials to posterity than they were back in the 1950s.

But the subsidy gets darker and goes much deeper. It also includes the lives of those who get sick and die prematurely because of exposure to radioactivity caused by the commercial nuclear industry, which includes radioactivity that every commercial reactor routinely emits. Fission by-products include strontium $^{90}$, iodine $^{131}$, cesium $^{137}$, argon, krypton, xenon, and whatever else. Most of these are gasses. These gasses must be continually stripped out and removed from primary water at all reactors and pumped into holding tanks, because they're radioactive. The thing that happens when gases continually get pumped into a holding tank, though, is that pressure inside the tank increases. So long as nuclear plants are operating, the pressure inside these holding tanks continues increasing until a designated pressure is reached, and then the gasses are isolated and as soon as a period of time deemed sufficient for radioactive decay has passed, the plant operators wait for the right weather parameters. Then, well before ten radioactive half-lives of some of these captured gasses passes, they get released to the atmosphere.

Radiation monitoring programs around nuclear power plants will tell plant operators when something breaks or when there are accidental radiation releases, but their monitoring is not designed or intended to monitor routine releases. The nuclear industry operates with the belief that radiation exposure from these releases is below regulatory concern. As a result, we have no knowledge of dispersion patterns of released radioactive gasses, or where they may accumulate in lower areas, or areas sheltered from the wind, or ravines along riverbanks, for example. Independent investigators, such as Dr. Ernest Sternglass, professor emeritus at the University of Pittsburgh and director of the Radiation and Public Health Project, documented the potential for significant public exposure to these releases and calculated the death and destruction they can cause. Dr. Sternglass was not alone. There was also Dr. Rosalie Bertell, Dr. Helen Caldicott, Dr. Judith Johnsrud and Joseph Mangano, and many more who did their best against an intransigent, rich and powerful murderous clique, to provide public information of the danger. The danger continues because without these releases of fission by-products, there could be no commercial nuclear power. So the industry and its regulators, with tacit support from polite society, such as it is, continue in denial regarding public health consequences of the routine operation of commercial nuclear power plants.

Analysis of data from the federal National Cancer Institute (NCI), however, points to a more troubling reality. The Monticello boiling water reactor, located about forty miles upstream of Minneapolis on the Mississippi River, is one of the oldest commercial reactors in the world. It came online in 1970 and is in Wright County, close to the Sherburne County line. Xcel Energy/NSP is proceeding to get it relicensed for the third time, which would allow it to operate until it is an unprecedented eighty years old. Joseph Mangano submitted testimony to the Nuclear Regulatory Commission during the relicensing proceeding in which he reviewed NCI data for Wright and Sherburne Counties and compared it to Minnesota state-wide data prior to 1970 and then roughly every ten years until 2020, with corroborating provisional data for 2021, 2022, and 2023. The NCI data submitted in Joseph Mangano's testimony included overall deaths per 100,000 people; all-cancer mortality per 100,000 people; and all-cancer mortality for children per 100,000 people.

In all three instances, the death rates in Wright and Sherburne Counties were significantly below the state average prior to and during the early years of Monticello nuclear operations, which makes sense for a relatively affluent population not far from the Twin Cities. In all three instances, however, from 1990 through 2023, death rates per 100,000 people rose above the Minnesota state average. The data examined by Joseph Mangano revealed that between 1972 and 2020, Wright and Sherburne Counties experienced 4,319 excess deaths, compared to the number of deaths it would have experienced had it been at the state average. Considering that there are ninety-four operating reactors in the US, it is reasonable to conclude that commercial nuclear operations in the United States are responsible for more than 360,000 premature deaths. Can you think of an appropriate name for an entity that causes the premature deaths of 360,000 people over a thirty-eight year period? What do you think would happen to such an entity after the police caught up to it?

Take note that according to the BEIR VII Report, (Biological Effects of Ionizing Radiation) published in 2006 by the National Academies of Sciences, there is no safe dose of radiation. Every exposure comes with a risk of cellular damage capable of causing mutations and cancers. The greater the exposure, the greater the risk, and just because nobody is tracking dispersion patterns from routine gaseous radioactive releases does not mean that nobody gets exposed and affected. Because there is no safe dose, and because routine releases distribute doses, it is certain that routine radioactive releases from nuclear power plants contribute significantly to the continually increasing incidents of cancers, mutations and unviable pregnancies that society is experiencing. Joseph Mangano's Monticello relicensing testimony, now in the public record, confirms this reality.

So, in America, with an offer from Cold Warriors that could not be refused, commercial nuclear reactors started joining the fleet of central station power plants owned and operated by power companies beginning in the late 1960s. For power companies, the technology was gifted. Liability for accidents was eliminated. Waste management was ultimately the federal government's problem, not theirs. And a blind eye is turned toward public health consequences of nuclear power. While the "too cheap to meter" part did not work out so well, without *each* of these massive subsidies, there could be no commercial nuclear power because in a free and fair market economy, commercial nuclear power cannot pay its own freight.

Beyond doubt, these subsidies are required to enable the operation of twenty percent of the US electric utility market, and beyond all doubt, they totally wipe out any semblance of free and fair energy markets. From this starting point, however, nuclear power's situation degenerates even deeper into absurdity when looking at just the installation costs for new nuclear capacity compared to renewable energy installation costs.

This absurdity was recognized in the Proceedings of the National Academy of Sciences in July 2018, whereby the authors concluded that fission power is just too expensive to gain traction going forward into the carbonless future. While we still see politicians at both the state and federal levels attempting a nuclear revival in the name of combating global warming, the fact is that nuclear power is **MUCH** too expensive, never mind the subsidies. The most recent new reactors to come online are at the Vogtle Plant outside of Augusta, Georgia, Unit 3 in 2023 and Unit 4 in March 2024. The installed cost for the new twin 1,215 MW nuclear reactors at Vogtle is upward of $13,000,000 per megawatt. The next fission reactors to come online, if that ever happens, will be even more expensive.

On the other hand, new solar capacity costs about $1,000,000 per megawatt to install, new wind capacity comes in around $2,000,000 per megawatt, and for $3 million, you can get a megawatt of storage capacity that will last about ten hours before needing to be recharged.

Warped economics permeate every aspect of commercial nuclear power and give rise to the dictum that anything is cheap if you do not pay for it. But warped economics is just one of many characteristics that illustrate the bizarre and twisted nature of the commercial nuclear power industry. As we delve into some of the physical aspects of this disturbing reality, it is necessary that we also shed some light upon the malignant human and social behavior that has not just accompanied nuclear power since its inception but enabled it.

As White people shot and bullied their way to dominance in North America, in Africa, and in Australia, the Indigenous Peoples living on these continents when White people arrived, those who survived, at least, tended to get shunted off to remote, marginal lands to make of it as best they could. Turns out, most of the world's uranium deposits are on remote, marginal lands. Uranium is mined and milled on Hopi, Navajo, Pueblo, and Cree Lands in North America, and on Aboriginal Homelands in Australia and South Africa. So, on the front end of the nuclear chain, with uranium mining being the primary employment "opportunity" in the communities that got shunted, many if not most of the men in those communities got abused with scurrilous labor practices until they died slowly, painfully and young as radiation protection procedures either did not exist, were ignored or were ineffectual. Mortality rates among uranium miners, driven by exposure to radon, were 380 percent higher than in the standard population. We continue living with the legacy as well as the practice of nuclear racism.

As miners dig uranium ore out of the ground, about 99.28 percent of it is $U^{238}$. But reactor fuel needs to be $U^{235}$ because $U^{235}$ has fewer protons and is therefore less stable than $U^{238}$. The instability of $U^{235}$ atoms is what enables a critical mass of them to initiate and sustain a chain reaction of exploding atoms, which is where the heat to boil the water comes from. So uranium enrichment is the next link in the nuclear fuel chain. Extracting $U^{235}$ from uranium ore is one of those dense industrial energy processes that requires big coal fires. The uranium ore gets heated to boiling, and because gaseous $U^{235}$ atoms are slightly smaller than gaseous $U^{238}$, centrifuges, over many millions of iterations, slowly isolates $U^{235}$ from the rest of it until you get to fuel grade, usually between three percent and five percent. Keep the centrifuges spinning and the iterations iterating, and you eventually get up to weapons-grade, which is about ninety percent $U^{235}$. Uranium enrichment creates numerous opportunities for releasing radioactive contamination into the environment.

Uranium enrichment is a primary connection that links the Cold Warriors with "Atoms for Peace." The technology required to enrich uranium ore to fuel grade $U^{235}$ is the same technology that enriches uranium up to weapons-grade $U^{235}$. The Cold Warriors reasoned, correctly, it turns out, that the American public would hardly notice the massive expenditure on the uranium enrichment technology that thermonuclear holocaust requires if that same technology could be used to make electricity too cheap to meter, even if it did not. In any event, while nuclear power plants do not emit greenhouse gases on-site, energy requirements of uranium enrichment cause nuclear power plants to be responsible for about ten percent of the carbon dioxide that would be emitted if coal, instead of $U^{235}$, were being used to boil water to produce the steam to generate equivalent amounts of electricity.

Fuel fabrication is the next link in the nuclear chain, whereby uranium enriched to between three percent and five percent $U^{235}$ gets fabricated into fuel pellets, each of which is about 3/8 inch in diameter and 5/8 inch in length. Nuclear fuel fabrication also creates numerous opportunities for radiological contamination of the environment, as Karen Silkwood discovered in the early 1970s. Ms. Silkwood worked for Kerr-McGee at a fuel fabrication plant in Oklahoma, where lax regulations and poor enforcement were causing radioactive contamination issues inside and outside the plant. She drew attention to the problem, and while on her way to expose the plant's negligent safety records, she died in a mysterious one-car crash on November 13, 1974. There's a movie about it.

During the mid-1990s NSP was a primary partner in a nuclear fuel fabrication company called Louisiana Energy Services (LES). LES intended to own and operate the world's first privately owned uranium enrichment plant. LES first chose a site for what it called a "chemical plant" in the local media, in a community with a population that was about twenty percent African American. That community organized and kicked LES out, so LES next went to a community with a popula-tion of about fifty percent Black, which also organized and kicked them out. After another similar experience in a community that was eighty percent African American, LES settled on Homer, Louisiana, which is about ninety-eight percent Black. Homer residents mobilized under the banner of Citizens Against Nuclear Trash (CANT), and fought back.

In response to the leadership of our local electric utility, NSP, in this horrifically racist and bigoted enterprise, as well as to all the other racist links in the nuclear chain, the North American Water Office and its allies organized an international conference, "Confronting Nuclear Racism" in 1995. We came out of our conference with a shareholder campaign intent on getting NSP to remove itself from the LES debacle. In the first year, we got about five percent of shareholder shares voting to withdraw. The second year, we got over ten percent and were on pace to put our own Director on the NSP Board, and then, before you could run through two percent of the half-life of tritium, NSP withdrew from LES, LES withdrew from Homer and CANT won out.

Anyway, these nuclear fuel pellets get stacked one on top of the other and are contained inside metal tubes that are about fourteen feet long. Tubes filled with pellets are fuel rods. These rods are bundled to-gether to form fuel assemblies, each of which consists of between about 80, up to 200 fuel rods, depending on the type of reactor, which brings us to nuclear power plants, the next link in the nuclear chain.

Prairie Island is an island close along the Minnesota side of the Mississippi River, about thirty miles southeast of Minneapolis/St. Paul, in Goodhue County and about six miles upstream from the City of Red Wing. It has been a place of deep cultural and spiritual significance to the Mdewakanton Dakota People since beginning in the mists of time, a beautiful, majestic place where elders came and then walked on. It is home for the Prairie Island Mdewakanton Dakota Nation. The people living there in 1960 were the grandchildren, great grandchildren and great great grandchildren of the people who got put there after the 1862 Indian War, caused by federal Indian Agents who told Dakota People being starved to death by the thieving agents, to "eat grass." At the end of the war, President Lincoln ordered the largest mass execution in American history, and on December 26, 1862, thirty-eight Dakota men were hung just outside of Mankato. After the war, the "good Indians," those who had not participated in the warring, got sent to Prairie Island.

In the 1960s, the local power company, Northern States Power (NSP, now Xcel Energy), told the Prairie Island Mdewakanton people that it was going to build a steam plant right next to their reservation. Then NSP sponsored grave digs, very publicly advertised, for anyone who was interested to show up at the site prior to construction and snoot around to see what they could find. After all, the whole area would just get torn up anyway. Then NSP built its steam plant on top of burial mounds.

When the good citizens of Red Wing realized that a power plant was coming, they quickly went to work and annexed the Prairie Island Community, never mind that Prairie Island is six miles upstream by river and in the '60s, close to half an hour away if you were having a medical emergency. But the annexation enabled the City of Red Wing to reap about $15 million a year in taxes from the plant, rather than wasting all that money on the Indians. In exchange, Red Wing provided the Prairie Island Community with a playground that had a very nice swing set and a little teeter-totter. These events occurred in the 1960s and early 1970s.

It turned out, of course, that exploding $U^{235}$ atoms inside a big, sealed up steel kettle would make the steam for NSP's steam plant. Unit I came online in 1973 and Unit 2 in 1974, twin 600 MW pressurized water reactors. From then on, the City of Red Wing and virtually all of the fine people who lived there and nearby around and about Goodhue County, became boisterous and vociferous supporters of NSP, the Prairie Island Nuclear Plant, and nuclear power in general, no matter what, with one exception, to which we will in due course get.

Fuel assemblies are designed so that when the big steel kettle is full of them, which at Prairie Island amounts to about 121, the self-sustaining chain reaction of exploding $U^{235}$ atoms occurs. To manage this chain reaction, control rods, which absorb exploded atomic particles, can be inserted into the core strategically, thereby reducing or stopping the chain reaction of atomic explosions, and controlling the production of heat required to keep the turbines spinning. Mostly, however, once they get started, nuclear reactors want to keep on running full-bore all the time, which is why they are called baseload plants. Once started, they will not stop until something breaks, or fuel assemblies need to get replaced. Then control rods get inserted into the core which interrupts the chain reaction, causing the reactors to shut down for maintenance and refueling. The ability of $U^{235}$ atoms to explode in a self-sustaining chain reaction, producing heat to flash water into steam to spin turbines to generate electricity begins to diminish after spending four or five years in a reactor core. Chunks of fission debris increasingly interfere with the chain reaction, so it slows down, and now you got your high-level nuclear waste, even though close to ninety-five percent of the $U^{235}$ atoms remain unexploded. To continue reactor operations, this spent irradiated waste must be removed from the reactor core and replaced with fresh fuel assemblies. Typically, about 1/3 of the 121 fuel assemblies in the Prairie Island reactor cores get replaced and become waste every eighteen months or so.

High-level nuclear waste management programs form the next links in the nuclear chain, and no one knows how many of these links will be required to manage the waste for the required period of time. We should clarify, however, that there are all sorts of nuclear waste streams attached to the commercial nuclear industry, everything from the clothes and tools worn and used by workers, and the rags they use to mop up spills, to worn out and broken power plant components and equipment. All of it is designated low-level waste, except for the irradiated fuel. There are innumerable issues and problems attached to the management of low-level nuclear waste streams, some of which are extremely hot, but we'll leave them for another time. For present purposes, the point is that irradiated fuel, and only irradiated fuel, is high-level nuclear waste.

This irradiated fuel waste is extremely hot, both thermally and in terms of radioactivity. It continues to generate lots of heat, and contains a host of very nasty radioactive materials, including cesium $^{137}$, strontium $^{90}$ and plutonium. When this waste gets removed from a reactor core, it is hot enough radioactively so that a single fuel rod, if it were unshielded and you were within ten feet of it, would deliver a lethal dose in less than a second. It must be isolated from biological activity while it cools. Seeing as how the half-life of plutonium is about 24,000 years, after applying the "rule of thumb," we are talking about a waste management program that must maintain its integrity pretty close to a geological period of time. (A radioactive half-life is the time it takes for half of the radioactivity of a given substance to dissipate. For example, the half-life of tritium is about twelve years. So after twenty-four years, it will be twnety-five percent as radioactive as it was in its beginning.)

Because the waste is so hot thermally as well as radioactively when it gets taken out of the reactor core, the period of isolation must begin under water in a storage pool. But the genius Cold Warriors who plotted out our nuclear future back then thought the waste would be reprocessed, which is vastly different from being recycled, so they did not make storage pools very big during the 1960s and into the 1970s. Reprocessing irradiated fuel, their reasoning went, would enable more of the remaining ninety-five percent of unexploded $U^{235}$ atoms to get refabricated back into fresh fuel assemblies, and then go back into a reactor core to boil more water.

But reprocessing irradiated fuel is a complicated, very messy process. The waste fuel rods get ground up and dissolved in big vats of acid, and then the dissolved solution gets processed to remove non-fissile fractions, and the fissile fraction gets refabricated into nuclear fuel pellets. By the late '70s, though, after much consternation, US decision makers figured out that reprocessing waste nuclear fuel enabled and encouraged proliferation of nuclear weapons, thereby making atomic and "dirty" bombs much more accessible to the "bad'uns." Also, lots of people living in the neighborhoods of reprocessing plants, like West Valley in New York, started dying young. So, the United States stopped trying to reprocess nuclear waste during the Carter administration.

Built to only hold irradiated fuel for six or seven years, just long enough for it to be cool enough thermally to allow it to be shipped for reprocessing, by 1978, the Prairie Island storage pool was filling up. So NSP asked for and got state governmental permission to re-rack the pool so that more waste could get crammed into the same space. I was otherwise occupied in 1978, but NSP needed to do this re-racking again a couple years later, and this time I was associated with a handful of people who formed the Prairie Island Project to challenge the second re-racking. A primary concern with re-racking, we quickly understood, is that each time the space between the spent fuel assemblies dangling from their racks in the storage pool gets reduced, safety margins get diminished as more very hot waste fuel assemblies get packed closer and closer together. We will examine potential consequences of these reduced safety margins in due course.

The Prairie Island Project got rolled, more waste got crammed into the pool, and safety margins were again reduced. But we learned a lot about nuclear power and all the links in the nuclear fuel chain, including that the second re-racking would still not be sufficient. NSP would come back for more high-level nuclear waste storage capacity before too long. We were watching, and sure enough, in 1987 NSP comes along with a proposal for "temporary" TN-40 dry storage casks, outdoors next to the plant, immediately adjacent to the Prairie Island Mdewakanton Dakota Nation, in the floodplain of the Mississippi River. NSP wanted forty-eight of them. TN stands for Transnuclear, the outfit that fabricates TN-40 casks, and forty is the number of waste fuel assemblies that fit inside a TN-40 cask.

The North American Water Office was ready and waiting for NSP to make its move. The fight started in 1987 when NSP submitted its Environmental Impact Statement (EIS) to state bureaucrats for the nuclear waste dump, which NSP and the bureaucrats called an Independent

Spent Fuel Storage Installation, an ISFSI. We challenged the adequacy of the EIS and won, so NSP had to amend and resubmit its EIS, which took a year. The amended version was as inadequate as the original, but the second time through, craven bureaucrats gave it a pass. We used the year, however, to organize against the dump with as much force and strength as we could muster and in conjunction with Prairie Island Mdewakanton Dakota tribal leadership, formed the Prairie Island Coalition Against Nuclear Storage (PICANS), which grew to include over thirty environmental, safe-energy, religious, student, labor and civic organizations. For the next six years, people in these organizations wrote tens of thousands of letters to editors, politicians and bureaucrats, attended hundreds of protests and rallies, and by the time the fight reached the Minnesota Legislature in 1994, they showed up *en masse* when needed to lobby politicians.

The acceptance of the EIS the second time around set the stage for an administrative proceeding to determine the need for 48 TN-40 casks on Prairie Island, and based on the evidence, PICANS won. After looking at all the facts presented during the proceeding which lasted about two months, the Administrative Law Judge (ALJ) reported to the Minnesota Public Utilities Commission (MPUC) that the risks of deploying TN-40 casks outweighed any societal benefit they would produce. "No casks," said the judge. We rejoiced. We partied! Then the decision went before the MPUC where the ALJ's recommendation was rejected, but the commission only authorized seventeen casks, not forty-eight. We cursed and ranted against this duplicitous behavior, and then we appealed the MPUC's decision to Minnesota's Appellate Courts where we won, because under Minnesota law, only the Minnesota Legislature has authority to site a permanent high-level nuclear waste storage facility in Minnesota.

Significantly, this nuclear waste law was passed in 1982, in the wake of the fight against the 800 kV DC powerline across West Central Minnesota, chronicled in *Powerline: The First Battle of America's Energy Wars* by US Senator Paul Wellstone and Dr. Barry Casper. At the time, the Federal Department of Energy was still trying to select a site for the nation's high-level nuclear waste repository, and the Granite Shield in Northern Minnesota was in the running, along with a portion of southwestern Minnesota. Powerline protesters did not like that idea any more than they liked the powerline, and because of the powerline fight, Minnesota politicians were sensitized to energy issues. The law therefore got passed in order to keep the Federal Department of Energy from attempting to site their high-level nuclear waste repository in Minnesota, and the law was successful because the DoE eventually settled on Yucca Mountain in Nevada as its repository site. But in 1993, after Minnesota *bureaucrats* on the Public Utilities Commission authorized seventeen storage casks for Prairie Island, we appealed.

Clearly, the Public Utilities Commission wasn't the legislature, so we asked the court, "If the ISFSI is 'temporary,' as NSP and the commission claim, where will the waste go, and when will it go there?" In response, NSP and the Commission could do no better than "somewhere else sometime," so the matter hinged on how long is "temporary." The court acknowledged precedence in that if a road or a building, for example, is around for seven years, it's considered to be "permanent." In 1993, there was no credible claim by anyone that there would be anywhere capable of accepting nuclear waste from Prairie Island within seven years, thereby making it a "permanent" dump in the eyes of the court. This ruling set the stage for the 1994 legislative fight that we lost, in that seventeen TN-40 casks on Prairie Island were authorized, but the terms and conditions attached to the authorization dragged NSP and the electric utility industry of North America into the Modern Era.

It also set the stage for an instructive display of social behavior that can occur when a community gets bought and paid for, as NSP did with the City of Red Wing and the good citizens of Goodhue County, who loved all things nuclear except for this time to which we have now in due course got. Part of the Prairie Island legislation that passed in 1994 required NSP to develop a high-level nuclear waste storage facility in Goodhue County, seeing as how most people living there strongly supported nuclear power, but off Prairie Island, because the people living there did not. When the site for the alternative dump site six miles down the Mississippi River, by Frontenac, was announced, Goodhue County residents showed up in droves to voice their vociferous opposition to the dump and organized themselves to defeat it. After making the most difficult decision of my life, I helped them organize in order to keep Minnesota from setting a precedent of scattering irradiated fuel around and about regardless of political purposes. I decided it was better to be a racist in the eyes of some, than to proliferate nuclear sacrifice zones. The alternative Goodhue County nuclear waste dump was abandoned after federal officials ruled that it would be more dangerous to ship the waste downriver six miles to Frontenac than it would be to ship it about 1,400 miles to a dump that was being proposed in Utah, about which we will discuss shortly.

This fight over Prairie Island nuclear waste only happened, however, because of the abysmal failure on the part of the Federal Department of Energy to keep its promise to the electric utility industry back when the Cold Warriors told power companies that the government was responsible for the waste. After all, if the government were accepting spent fuel as it promised, there would have never been a need for dry storage casks on Prairie Island.

Once it became clear in the late 1970s that reprocessing irradiated fuel would not be happening, the attention of the Federal Department of Energy's high-level nuclear waste management program had to shift its attention to focus on establishing a national permanent deep geological repository. By 1982, the search for a site was underway and included potential sites in Texas and Washington State, as well as Minnesota, before deciding in 1987 that Yucca Mountain in Nevada would be the nation's only permanent, high-level nuclear waste repository site. The Nevada site was chosen not for any particular intrinsic suitability reasons, but because it was Nevada, sparsely populated and the place least likely to mount much popular opposition. Besides, it's in Indian Country.

It did not turn out the way the feds intended. Yucca Mountain is located on the ancestral lands of the Western Shoshone Nation, which to this day, having never surrendered to the US Government, maintains its sovereignty and remains adamantly opposed to the dump. Efforts to develop the dump were therefore in violation of the 1863 Treaty of Ruby Valley between the Western Shoshone Nation and the US Government, in yet another example of nuclear racism. Further, Yucca Mountain sits atop the Ghost Dance Fault, which experienced a 5.7 magnitude earthquake in 1992, not quite in time for our hearing before the ALJ. Standing on top of Yucca Mountain, you can see three volcanic cinder cones in the valley immediately to the west, and the mountain itself is composed of porous volcanic tuff, so there are no natural barriers preventing nuclear contamination from spreading off-site as soon as the corrosive water percolating through the tuff corrodes through casks storing waste, which would be relatively soon compared to the required 240,000 year period of isolation until the waste is relatively benign.

Intrinsic problems with the Yucca Mountain site, corrupt science as the federal government and the nuclear industry characterized the site, and tenacious resistance to the dump by the Western Shoshone Nation, the people of Nevada and the anti-nuclear movement ultimately killed the Yucca proposal in 2010, at least for a while. But late in 1991, government and industry witnesses swore under oath that Yucca Mountain would certainly be accepting high-level nuclear waste no later than 2020, and that the Federal Department of Energy would absolutely be accepting title to the waste, as it was by law required to do, by 1998. That part about the feds accepting title to the waste sounded good and contributed to the illusion of progress toward an operational high-level nuclear waste dump, but doing so had absolutely no effect whatsoever regarding where nuclear waste gets stored, or timelines regarding the development of storage facilities.

Even in 1991, it was apparent to any non-jaded observer, including the ALJ, what is still true over thirty years later, namely, that as deadlines for achieving milestones toward an operational high-level nuclear waste management program came and went, the exact date by which such a program might actually be accepting irradiated fuel from the nation's fleet of commercial nuclear reactors receded further into a distant and increasingly foggy and uncertain future. In any event, Yucca Mountain was not available in 1991, and there were no other off-site alternatives for storing Prairie Island waste. Putting the waste into storage casks on Prairie Island was the NSP and State of Minnesota response to the nuclear industry's need to fill the gap in time until they purported that Yucca Mountain would become operational, hence the "temporary" nature of their proposition. Without dry cask storage on Prairie Island, the reactors would be forced to shut down.

At the federal level, the primary response to this time-gap was to embark in 1991 on what they called the "Monitored Retrievable Storage" (MRS) program. The MRS program sought to find a central-ized high-level nuclear waste storage site where waste from reactors all across the country could be shipped and stored in many thousands of casks until the Yucca Mountain Repository was ready to accept it. The MRS program got started by the Federal Department of Energy send-ing out a letter to each of the 3,141 or so county, or county equivalents of local government in the entire US of A. Every tribal government in the nation also got a letter. The letter offered each of these local units of government $100,000 of taxpayer money that they would use to in-form people in their community about how good it would be for them if they agreed to put thousands of dry storage casks full of high-level nuclear waste somewhere in their back yard, and keep it there until it could be shipped somewhere else, like to Yucca Mountain.

Four county governments requested the $100,000. The county commissioners in one of those four were simply impeached and re-moved from office on the spot. The commissioners in the other three were not re-elected, and that was the end of that for predominantly white communities. But seventeen tribal governments responded, most with the stated intent of providing "economic development opportunities" for their people. In America, we encourage the most disenfranchised among us to manage our most heinous wastes, thus illustrating another aspect of nuclear racism, of which by now you know, there are many.

Interestingly enough, the Prairie Island Mdewakanton Dakota Nation was one of the seventeen, reasoning that being as NSP and the state were intent on dumping high-level nuclear waste in casks immediately adjacent to the Tribe no matter what, the Tribe might as well take the money from the feds and use it to inform the community about what was coming. They got the money, and then, in a strategic coup for the ages, they contracted with the North American Water Office to administer their MRS program. With direction provided by the Tribal Council, NAWO used that $100,000 from the federal government to inform not just the Prairie Island Community, but the whole entire state and a big chunk of western Wisconsin about costs and benefits of interim dry cask storage of irradiated fuel on Prairie Island. What a hoot! We made our good friend Senator Paul Wellstone proud.

That left sixteen tribal governments all set up with slick nuclear industry and government propaganda about all the jobs an MRS dump would provide, and how much money it would bring into the community, and how safe it would all be, how all the waste would be gone to Yucca Mountain before too long, and how an aesthetically pleasing and well designed and managed facility might actually become a tourist destination. Fortunately, significant numbers of tribal members in each of those communities, led by Grace Thorpe (Jim Thorpe's daughter) and the National Environmental Coalition of Native Americans (NECONA), were not buying the bullkaka. And the Indigenous Environmental Network (IEN), led by Tom Goldtooth, provided an extremely valuable organizational and educational venue to counter the propaganda.

In the Spring of '92, shortly after the ALJ's "No Casks on Prairie Island" Recommendation but before the Public Utilities Commission overturned the ALJ's recommendation, IEN sponsored a conference to deal with this MRS attack on Indian Country. People from across the continent and around the world, including representatives of each of the seventeen responding tribes were invited, along with an impressive list of nuclear experts. Several hundred people showed up to figure out how to deal with the MRS problem. The conference was about a hundred miles up the Columbia River from Portland. I was asked to come and share information both about the strategy NAWO and the Prairie Island Tribe were developing to manage the $100,000 MRS grant, and about what PICANS had learned regarding dry cask storage of high-level nuclear waste during the course of the proceeding before the ALJ.

The IEN Conference was instrumental in causing all but two of the Tribes to back away from the MRS program, and set the foundation for organizing that eventually, more than a decade later, would totally kill the MRS program. Tribal leadership first in the Mescalero Apache Nation in New Mexico and then in the Skull Valley Goshutes Nation in Utah, tried hard to get MRS facilities on their reservations, and in both instances, tenacious and persistent community opposition supported by organizations like IEN, NECONA and NAWO ultimately defeated those attempts.

Truth be told, however, we had some help from the US Air Force regarding the deal in Utah. The Skull Valley Band of Goshutes Reservation is located about seventy miles south and west of the Great Salt Lake. The land is spectacular, but it is desert, and the tribal lands are immediately adjacent and to the east of the Utah Test and Training Range, where pilots from Hill Air Force Base test their skills and their ordinance. It took the generals in charge the better part of a decade, but they finally figured out that it would probably not be prudent to have their fighter jets screeching along fifty feet above the ground at Mach 1.6 and flying over thousands of tons of irradiated fuel on their way to dropping 500-pound bombs during target practice. Why it took the brass so long to figure that out remains an interesting question, but the MRS program failed to find a site for centralized dry cask storage of high-level nuclear waste.

In the United States, dry cask storage remains the only option for managing waste assemblies that must be evacuated from storage pools to make room for irradiated fuel waste fresh from reactor cores. Without this evacuation, reactors will have no option other than to shut down. So, more casks are getting filled up with irradiated fuel at reactor sites across the country regardless of the prudence of having such a dangerous material scattered around and about the country. As of this writing, there are fifty TN-40 casks on Prairie Island.

Faced with governmental failure, in recent years, cask manufacturers have been trying to get in on the action by designing and operating their own high-level nuclear waste storage facilities. An outfit called Holtec International is attempting to site a 100,000 metric ton storage facility, recently rebranded Consolidated Interim Storage (CIS), adjacent to Hispanic communities in Eastern New Mexico. Once again, fierce opposition got organized and fought back, and this time, even oil and gas companies got involved as they feared an incident at the storage facility could ruin their ability to pump oil. Also, the proposed site sits atop the Ogallala Aquifer, by far the primary source of water out there in the desert. The opposition was successful, at least for now, and on or about March 28, 2024, the federal courts blocked Holtec from proceeding with its dump. What the ultimate fate of the waste coming out of reactor cores will be, therefore, remains an open question. Reprocessing is out, Yucca Mountain has been abandoned, and after thirty years of trying, the nuclear industry still has no centralized high-level nuclear waste cask storage facility, and no prospect of having one anytime soon.

As of this writing, there is no federal repository program, although some politicians are grumbling about Yucca Mountain again. There is no centralized waste storage facility, and there will be no such facilities in the foreseeable future. So the waste keeps piling up in casks at reactor sites, creating a whole additional set of problems. Part of this new set has to do with the fact that some types of storage casks, such as the TN-40, are not designed for transporting irradiated fuel. They are too big and heavy, and the waste dangling down into the cask cavity is not adequately supported for the rigors of transportation. It is, after all, a *storage* cask. Transport casks are different. There are also duel-purpose casks, deemed suitable for storage and transport, but the TN-40 is not one of them.

Before irradiated fuel in TN-40 casks can be transported, it must be removed from the TN-40 and placed into a transport cask. Because the fuel assemblies will still be extremely radioactive, this transfer must take place either under water, back in the storage pool, or in a very expensive "hot cell" into which both the TN-40 and the transport cask are placed, and a very complicated transfer is made robotically. Actual protocol for an underwater transfer does not yet exist and could be complicated by thermal shock as waste assemblies get reimmersed, and both scenarios assume that the waste assemblies have maintained their integrity and remain intact. There are several degradation modes that challenge this assumption, including metal embrittlement and corrosion if even a few molecules of water remained in the cask as it was initially loaded and sealed. If fuel assembly degradation has occurred, which could include warped and twisted fuel rods, or fuel cladding degraded to the extent that fuel pellets fall to the bottom of a cask, new procedures and protocols will need to be identified. But what if enough cladding degenerates inside a cask so that fuels pellets accumulate on the bottom in a pattern that goes critical?

On a more philosophical note, what hubris is required to create waste that must be isolated from biological activity for 240,000 years, and to then pretend that humans have the ability to implement a management program capable of doing so?

So far, we have examined some of the issues and challenges that confront the commercial nuclear industry when everything's working the way it's supposed to work. All too often, however, they do not. Something breaks. Something got overlooked, last week or fifty years ago. Somebody screws up. With any other electrical generation technology, when something untoward happens, you shut it down, assess the damage and fix it. Unless your untoward incident involves a coal ash pile getting washed into a river, chances are good that the damage is limited to situations within the power plant's boundaries. Not so with nuclear power. Nuclear technologies are terribly unforgiving, as attested, for example, by explosions at Fukushima and Chernobyl, the partial meltdown at Three Mile Island, and the industry's complete dependence on the indemnification provided by the Price-Anderson Act.

Also, we almost lost Detroit.

In 1963, the Enrico Fermi Nuclear Generating Station located next to Lake Erie near Detroit came online. Fermi was a "breeder" reactor in which the core gets cooled by liquid sodium. A given volume of liquid sodium can absorb much more heat than water, enabling the core to be denser than a water-cooled reactor. This density causes the chain-reaction of exploding $U^{235}$ atoms to convert $U^{238}$, which is about ninety-five to ninety-seven percent of the uranium in the core, into plutonium$^{239}$, which can be fabricated into reactor fuel. Hence the "breeder" label, and proclamations of a "limitless" supply of fuel.

But on October 5, 1966, clogged up pipes prevented liquid sodium from circulating through the core, things quickly heated up, and the core began to melt. Frantic activity got the pipes unplugged, with minutes to spare before a molten mass of fuel accumulated at the bottom of the reactor core and went critical. Had that happened, the nuclear reaction would have been unstoppable, as there would have been no way to smother it with concrete, as happened with devastating consequences at Chernobyl. Water will act like liquid fuel in such a conflagration. The mass of molten fuel would have burned its way through the floor of the containment structure until it struck groundwater, and the resulting intensely radioactive steam explosions would have likely caused the evacuation and abandonment of Detroit. A loss-of-coolant event at any one of the nation's 94 reactors could result in a similar need to evacuate and abandon a very large area. We came really close to such an event at many, if not most, of the nation's sixty-three pressurized water reactors, as acknowledged by the Nuclear Regulatory Commission on March 4, 1996, in its news-letter "Inside NRC," Vol. 18, No.5.

It turned out that while the cheating, lying, amok-running thieves over at Northern States Power Company (NSP, now Xcel Energy) were telling Minnesota decision-makers in 1994 about how good their Prairie Island (PI) nuclear reactors were, hence the need for dry cask storage of high-level nuclear waste, they were also preparing to sue Westinghouse Electric Corp. in Minnesota's US Federal District Court because the PI nuclear steam generators sold to NSP by Westinghouse were prematurely aging, corroding, cracking, leaking and threatening massive, catastrophic uncontrolled radiation releases. NSP waited until the dust started to settle after our fight over nuclear waste storage ended on the last day of the 1994 Minnesota Legislative Session, and a few days later it filed its suit against Westinghouse.

Despite the fact that NSP was the thirteenth electric utility company to sue Westinghouse because of the faulty equipment Westinghouse was peddling, the general public as well as virtually all local, state, and federal leaders and authorities were blissfully oblivious of the reality surrounding the lawsuits, and equally oblivious of the accompanying threat posed by the mounting potential for catastrophic nuclear steam generator failure. All these authorities and somebodies were oblivious because of the way it worked legally. As soon as each of the first twelve lawsuits were filed in their local Federal District Court, the suing utility and Westinghouse would also move, together, for a Protective Order, which the courts would grant. The Protective Order would allow the two parties to share with each other all their pertinent documents regarding how much it would cost Westinghouse to resolve the matter, but it would prevent everybody else from seeing any of it. Behind the Protective Order, only the parties themselves were allowed to learn anything about the nature of the lawsuits or the negotiations.

Once the Protective Order was established, secretive negotiations between Westinghouse and the utility would begin. A trial date would be set by the court, but Westinghouse and the suing utility would negotiate as long as required to come to an agreement as to cost of the damage inflicted by faulty Westinghouse equipment on the suing utility, with the trial date delayed as often as necessary while negotiations continued, and negotiations continued until the day before the date on which the trial was set to begin.

Then, on the eve of trial, where the information would become public in open court, Westinghouse and the power company suing Westinghouse would announce that they had reached a Settlement Agreement and part of the Agreement was that the Protective Order would continue to prevent everyone except the parties to the suit from knowing anything about the nature of the problem, or its resolution. The power company would get a check from Westinghouse for several hundred million dollars, Westinghouse would get to wear an embarrassing grin, and nobody else would be the wiser. Ralph Nader and his organization, Public Citizen, along with others, tried repeatedly to crack through Protective Orders and get access to information that formed the substance of the cases, and failed every time. So, nobody except for Westinghouse and the suing power companies had any idea about what was actually going on.

But what was going on, by the early 1990s, was a mounting potential for cataclysmic steam generator tube ruptures which would result in catastrophic radiation releases that were poised to transform *thousands* of square miles surrounding every single one of the 60-some pressurized water reactors operating in the good old US of A, into abandoned sacrifice zones.

As noted, our nuclear waste fight with NSP began in 1987 and included the formation of the Prairie Island Coalition Against Nuclear Storage (PICANS). Devastated though PICANS was in the spring of 1994 by the fact that pretend democracy would now allow NSP to dump irradiated fuel in storage casks immediately adjacent to the Prairie Island Mdewakanton Dakota Community, when NSP filed its Westinghouse lawsuit shortly thereafter, the people who had formed the hard core of PICANS took a deep breath and shifted gears to confront this next threat. After all, the failure of a nuclear steam generator had potential, we suspected, to cause even more grievous harm than irresponsible nuclear waste management, at least in the shorter term. As we would learn, this harm could be unleashed at any moment.

But we already knew that steam generator tubes could rupture. We had direct experience of that on November 16, 1979, with a rupture event at Prairie Island. Sirens went off inside the plant as pressure relief valves opened, releasing radioactive steam into the atmosphere. Scores of plant personnel dashed frantically out the doors of the plant to the parking lot and drove with reckless abandon through the Prairie Island Reservation and off the island as fast as they could go, while tribal members watched with puzzlement. It wasn't until some hours later that radiation alarms went off and there was public notification of the event. According to the US Nuclear Regulatory Commission, NUREG/CR-6365, pages 84-85, by 1995 there had been fourteen tube ruptures in the United States.

Nuclear steam generators in pressurized water reactors like those at Prairie Island, are massive cylindrical-like structures inside the power plant's containment vessel. Prairie Island has four steam generators, two for each of its two units. Steam generators have big pipes that connect them to the reactor core, through which super-hot water circulates from the core, through the steam generator and back to the core. Steam generators stand up to seventy feet tall, weigh up to 800 tons, and are packed with thousands of relatively thin-walled inverted-U shaped tubes sealed up inside an otherwise mostly hollow steel casing. These tubes are made of a nickel/chromium alloy called Inconel because making them from Inconel is cheaper than making them from stainless steel, as the US Navy does for the tubes in the pressurized water reactors that power its nuclear fleet. Unfortunately, Inconel is also a lot more prone to various sorts of degradation. More on Inconel tubes shortly.

Steam generators get installed next to the reactor core, in which uranium$^{235}$ atoms are busy exploding in chain reactions caused by ultra-high-speed collisions with debris from other nearby exploding uranium[235] atoms. These chain reaction explosions produce fantastical amounts of heat, driven by the fact that the mass of a fuel pellet, which weighs about ten grams, gets multiplied by about 90,000,000,000,000 which is the speed of light in meters per second squared, to tell you how much energy a fuel pellet contains. So, a ten gram fuel pellet contains about as much energy as a ton of coal. Given that each fuel assembly weighs about 500,000 grams, and that there are 121 fuel assemblies with their U[235] atoms exploding away inside of each of the Prairie Island reactor cores when the plants are operating, and you can almost understand why society's infatuation with things nuclear tends to overwhelm the downside.

Anyway, all that heat gets absorbed by what is called "primary water" which circulates through the reactor core to the steam generator, where it transfers the heat to "secondary water" flowing through the steam generators on the other side of the Inconel tubes. After transferring the heat, the primary water circulates from the steam generators back to the reactor core to get reheated. If primary water were to stop removing heat from the exploding U[235] atoms in the reactor core, the core would have a meltdown, but we'll get to that in a bit. Even though that circulating primary water is upward of 600° F, it does not boil because it is pressurized upward of 1,200 psi, which is why they are called "pressurized water reactors," as opposed to "boiling water reactors" of Fukushima fame, which is what General Electric was selling and what NSP bought and installed at Monticello.

As the primary water gets pumped through the thousands of thin-walled Inconel tubes inside the steam generator, the heat gets transferred to secondary water getting pumped through the hollow cavity of the steam generator where contact with the 600+° F exterior walls of the Inconel tubes causes it to flash into steam. While the primary water gets pumped back to the core to be reheated, the expanding steam on the secondary side forces itself through a big pipe at very high pressure to a nozzle that directs it at the turbine which it spins, thereby causing the electric generator to generate electricity. Then the spent steam secondary water leaves the turbine and hits the condenser, where it condenses from steam back to liquid water, and then gets pumped back into the steam generator where it flashes into steam again to spin the turbine some more, gets condensed again and pumped back to the steam generator where it again flashes into steam to spin the turbine. There's a tertiary water pathway that takes water from the adjacent river, lake, or ocean, and runs it through the secondary track of the condenser to condense the steam in the secondary reactor loop back to water. Then the tertiary water running through the secondary track of the condenser gets dumped back into the river, lake or ocean at a considerably elevated temperature and laced with radioactive tritium, which creates a whole new set of issues. That is how it's all supposed to work, anyway.

The problem was that the thousands of Inconel tubes in each steam generator were experiencing stresses that were, evidently, beyond engineering specifications when the power plants were designed. There is thermal stress every time a reactor shuts down for maintenance and refueling and then starts up again, causing the metal to contract and expand, which, over time, can lead to metal fatigue. There is stress from sludge that builds up in crevices, where the tubes are joined to the metal plate at the base of the steam generator. That's where debris accumulates, causing corrosion and pitting. If you have a metal pot with a metal handle connected to it, the little crack between the pot and the handle is a crevice. Chances are really good that your pot's crevice is a darker color than the pot or the handle, and the stuff making the darker color is debris, and over time, debris results in corrosion.

There is fretting wear where tubes contact antivibration bars, and there is tube support plate thinning. Tubes get dented where they intersect support plates. There was stress during fabrication in the Inconel metal where the tubes got bent into their U shape, particularly with the inner tubes closer to the center of the steam generator where the U shape is the tightest. Chemical imbalances in primary or secondary water enhance Inconel tube cracking, but this also gets more compli-cated because while lithium and/or pH adjustments to primary and/or secondary water might decrease Inconel tube cracking, depending on levels of fuel crud and radiation fields, those same adjustments also in-crease corrosion of the Zircaloy cladding of the fuel rods in the reactor core. What to do, what to do. Where is the optimum regime? To some degree, there's also metal embrittlement caused by radiation exposure.

Over time, all these stress factors created little cracks in the Inco-nel tubes and where the hot and cold legs of the tubes were welded to the tubesheet, the metal plate with holes to hold the tubes in it, located toward the base of the steam generator. There was what they called "intergranular attack and stress corrosion cracking" (IGA/SCC) in the tubesheet crevice region. There were apex cracks in the tight inner U-bends. There were frequent but irregular tangential cracks running parallel to the tubes, with concentrations of these tangential cracks inside dented intersections with support plates. Of greatest concern were circumferential cracks which tended to occur at the tubesheet, by support plates and next to antivibration bars. If a tangential crack ruptured, a jet of primary water amounting to maybe five percent up to perhaps twenty or thirty percent of the water flowing through the tube would escape and flash to steam on the secondary side. But if a circumferential crack ruptured, 100 percent of the water flowing into that tube would get out.

Barring tube ruptures, primary water leaks relatively slowly out of those cracks into the secondary water. The way the powerplant opera-tors determined just how bad the leakage was, was to measure radio-activity in the secondary water, because, coming in direct contact with the core, the primary water was much more radioactive than second-ary water. When the radioactivity in the secondary water got too high, they knew they were leaking too much. Then they'd shut the sucker down and send probes that emitted electronic signals through each of the tubes, and when a probe came upon a crack or a dent or a pit, the recording of the electronic signal would be altered in such a way so that the operators could identify the location and magnitude of the degradation. When a particular tube got too cracked up, if they could, they would insert a sleeve and weld it into place. If the tube was too far gone, they would plug it and take that tube out of commission. By July 1992, one of the PI steam generators had almost 160 tubes plugged, which amounted to about five percent of its tubes, and combined, the four PI steam generators needed to have somewhere around forty tubes plugged per year.

The problem there, of course, was that every time a tube got plugged, the thermal exchange efficiency of the steam generator declined a bit, and the plugging had been going on long enough to start seriously reducing capacity factors – the amount of power produced by the plant as a fraction of how much the plant would produce if it were operating at full capacity all the time. The other problem was that every time plant workers dispatched their probes, or sleeved or plugged tubes, they got a healthy dose of radiation, which of course is not healthy.

Anyway, declining capacity factors and escalating steam generator maintenance costs reduced power company profits, and the power companies thought it was Westinghouse's fault that their profits were being unfavorably impacted. Hence the lawsuits and the Protective Orders and secret Settlement Agreements, and as noted, NSP's was the thirteenth electric utility to go to Court and try this stunt. But then things changed.

There we were, in US Federal court, District of Minnesota, Justice James Michael Rosenbaum presiding. The three of us, Ken Tilsen, movement attorney for the ages, Bruce Drew, World Class Statistician, chemical engineer, and Member of the NAWO Board of Directors, and myself were sitting on a courtroom bench behind the bar. Before the judge at one of the council tables up in front of the bar sat NSP's lawyers. At the other table sat Council for Westinghouse. And glaring down at both of them from his seat on high, Judge Rosenbaum said, "Every once in a while, a case comes before this Court in which you can just hear the litigants snarling at each other. This," he said as he sneered down first at one table and then at the other, wearing a smile worn by people very comfortable with their power, "is such a case."

At which point Ken stood up from where we were in the back behind the bar, with his right arm half extended and his index finger pointed toward the heavens, and loudly said, "But Your Honor! If these parties are resorting to this public forum to settle their private differences, then the public," he emphatically stated, "has a right to know the nature of those differences!"

As the litigants' heads spun in whiplash unison to look back at who had just bombed their altercation, the silence of the pause in the courtroom was palpable.

Several pregnant moments later, Judge Rosenbaum, looking over the top of his glasses past the puzzled litigants and squarely at Ken with us behind the bar, nodded and said, "I agree. An order to that effect will be issued." And with that, court was adjourned. Well now. We were in. We had won the right to participate in the discovery process. This had never happened before. Judge Rosenbaum's decision meant that we could review and learn about all the documents Westinghouse and NSP were exchanging between themselves to determine just what the physical damages to the Prairie Island Power Plant were, and how much Westinghouse would have to pay to settle those damages. The judge retired to his chambers and prepared his order establishing our rights to discovery.

Seeing as how NSP's pressurized water reactors were down at Prairie Island, which was of necessity where NSP did all its steam generator inspections, maintenance and analyses, that is also where NSP kept all the pertinent papers it would use to prepare for negotiating a settlement agreement. The papers were in an auxiliary single-story prefab-type office building inside plant security and adjacent to the power plant itself. So, the next day, Ken, Bruce and myself, along with three or four others, caravanned the thirty miles or so down US Highway 61 from the Twin Cities to Prairie Island. We got checked in through security and were ushered into a fairly large open office space in this auxiliary building where the documents we needed to examine were waiting for us.

"Where are the documents?" we politely asked.

"They are in those rooms back there," the presiding office worker waiting for us politely responded, pointing down a long hallway that ran the length of the building. Also in the room, the security detail assigned to us eyed us with suspicion. "You may go select a box and bring it to me so that I can make a record of the box you have," continued the office worker, "and then you may take the box to those tables," he pointed "over there, and look at its contents. When you are done with the box, bring it back to me," he concluded as he sat down behind a desk and watched us go to work.

There were several rooms full of boxes. Certainly, many hundreds, maybe over a thousand boxes. Your standard "Banker Box 785." As we discovered shortly, each box had somewhere in the neighborhood of 3,000-4,000 pages in it. Each page, every single page, had a unique number at the bottom called a "Bates Number." Each Bates Number was four digits, followed by a dash, followed by four more digits, although often they did not bother with the dash. Eight digits. Every page.

Where to start. So we walked down the hall to the first room, picked up a box and took it to the office person. We asked the office person if there was perhaps some index or filing system we might take a look at. The office person politely professed ignorance of any index or guide to the content of the boxes while recording the Bates Number of the first and last pages of our box. Then we took it to a table where we gathered round to see what we could see, and as a couple of us started taking random notes and recording Bates Numbers, the rest of us went back down the hall to get a couple more boxes, any box, at random, got them cleared by the office person, carried them over to a table, and then sat down to start taking random notes and recording Bates Numbers. None of us were very sure at all about precisely what it was we were looking at, or what we were looking for.

Bruce was the first to articulate a clue. "Look for pages," he told us, "that describe or illustrate some sort of tube degradation, and tubes that they plugged." Duh.

With that for guidance, when the office person told us politely five or six hours later that it was time to stop for the day, we had reviewed parts of several boxes, and everybody had a list with varying numbers of Bates-identified pages that described or discussed a variety of issues associated with the NSP v. Westinghouse lawsuit. We were way overwhelmed by the sheer volume of documents we needed to understand, but at least we had started, and could begin grappling with the magnitude of this challenge we had worked so hard to face. Before we got in our cars to drive back to the Twin Cities, we talked about several additional people we could invite to join us for day two of discovery and agreed to meet in this very same parking lot just outside the Security Gate the next morning to continue our effort.

We got up bright and early the next morning and eight or ten of us assembled in the parking lot by the Security Gate to present ourselves so the guards could let us in to continue our discovery work. Imagine our surprise when the guard asked, "Which one of you is George Crocker?"

I pled guilty.

"You're listed here as a security threat. You cannot enter the facility. Neither can they," he said, indicating my co-conspirators, "because they're with you."

"There must be some mistake," I replied politely.

"No mistake," said the guard. "Your name is on this list."

"Now just a minute here," said I, "At NSP's invitation, I've actually toured this plant several times in the past couple years," I continued, "and I've had the pleasure of touring your Becker plants and Monticello as well," which was totally true. "And just yesterday, myself and most of these people here," I said, indicating our team, "spent the entire working day in that building over there," I said, pointing to the auxiliary building, "reviewing documents that Federal Judge Rosenbaum's Court Order says we're entitled to review. So just how is it that we were okay to go in there to review documents yesterday, but not today?"

"I don't know anything about any of that," the guard responded. "I just know that you are on this list, which means that you are not allowed to enter this facility."

"How can this be?" "What's going on here, anyway?" "Why is this happening," we protested and complained as the situation momentarily escalated. This being day two, with day one having established precedence, we had presumed that Ken, our Attorney Extraordinaire and busy Law Professor at Hamline University, was not needed and instead was attending to other duties, so we were on our own.

We exchanged a few more pleasantries with the guard, who remained adamant in his insistence that I and therefore all we of us were a threat to the power plant, and so muttering and grumbling, we left the parking lot to find a phone (this was still a bit before the onslaught of modern electronic devices) at the Bingo Hall (prior to Treasure Island Resort & Casino), where we called Ken to inform him of our unexpected travails.

"Don't worry," Ken told us, "Just come on back and we'll see what the judge has to say about it." So back to town we went.

We were again in Federal District Court before Judge Rosenbaum within a few days. Only this time, NSP and Westinghouse were not sitting at opposing tables snarling at each other. Instead, Bruce and myself and Ken were at one of the council tables before the bar, and at the other sat NSP and Westinghouse, and they were not alone. Also at their table was INPO, the Institute of Nuclear Power Operators, a VERY HIGHLY secretive trade association of electric utilities that operate nuclear power plants, and EPRI, the Electric Power Research Institute, an electrical power research institution of which just about every electric power utility in the nation is a member. You can get their monthly publication, *The EPRI Journal,* if you want.

After all the parties to the proceeding, including INPO and EPRI noted their appearances for the record, Judge Rosenbaum said something to the effect of "Well now. Isn't this getting interesting?" after which Ken was asked to proceed.

"Well, Your Honor," he began, "a few days ago, I was with my clients down at the Prairie Island facility. We went through plant security and were escorted to an office building where we proceeded to exercise our rights of discovery, as per your order. Then, the following day," Ken continued, "while I remained in the Cities to perform other duties, my clients again presented themselves to plant security to continue our discovery process. Only this time, they were refused entry on the grounds they posed a security threat."

Ken continued to explain how preposterous this was and was just getting to the point of telling the judge about how in the recent past, NSP had actually *invited* Mr. Crocker to tour the plant, when the judge cut him off.

"I don't care about that," said Judge Rosenbaum gruffly. "It's NSP's job to decide who is a security threat and who isn't, not yours or mine. If NSP decides that Mr. Crocker is a security threat, then NSP has every right to protect its facilities from Mr. Crocker by denying him access to its facilities. But that has nothing to do with *this* case. I have already established that you and your clients, including Mr. Crocker, have a right to review the documents. Therefore," the judge decreed, "if NSP does not allow your clients, including Mr. Crocker, to review the documents in this matter at the facility at which they are currently located, NSP shall move those documents to a location at which your clients can review them."

Then the judge asked NSP, Westinghouse, INPO and EPRI if they understood. Unhappily, they said they did. "It is so ordered," concluded the judge and court was adjourned. Well now. Talk about cutting off your nose to spite your face. What was NSP thinking? Within a couple days, NSP had rented out a couple of rooms up toward the top of the 1st Bank Building in beautiful Downtown St. Paul, where we would go to continue our discovery. From these rooms we had a wonderful view looking north at the traffic on I-35E. Doing the work to organize and coordinate our discovery effort in these rooms in St. Paul was soooo much easier and cheaper and more efficient timewise than having to travel all the way down to Prairie Island, day after day. What a hoot.

Bruce took charge of the effort. We had access to the rooms from 9:00 a.m. to 4:30 p.m. five days a week. In one room was a desk and a chair behind the desk, and on the chair sat an NSP guy on guard duty. In the other room were piles and stacks of boxes. For the first couple of days, our core team showed up in the morning, cleared security without issue, went and got a box from the back room, plunked it down on the desk of the office guard duty guy who duly recorded Bates Numbers. Then we took them over to tables with chairs that we had procured to begin making sense of what we were looking at, and what we were looking for.

We quickly realized we would need a lot more people working on this if we were to get anywhere near through even half the boxes in a timely fashion. So, we helped Bruce organize a small army of about forty people to show up for half a day, or a full day if they could, five or six at a time, on a rotating basis, for the duration. When new people showed up, Bruce guided them through an organized orientation, and then they went and got a box, reported it to the guard duty guy, and went to work. Bruce also designed forms for all of us to use. The forms had a place for Bates Numbers and space to write a brief description of what the page or pages contained. Once we had a handle on what the more valuable information was, it quickly became apparent that we needed to make copies of the pages that described not only the various types of tube degradation and tube plugging, but also scientific papers discussing the variety of technical and scientific issues, management directives specifying how the litigation should proceed, memos attempting to define what the public face of all of this contention should be, and so forth and so on. So Bruce's form also had a box to identify the Bates Numbers of the pages with information that seemed to be important enough for us to copy.

We ordered a copy machine and had it delivered.

"Not so fast," said the NSP guard security guy as he blocked the delivery person attempting to wheel our copy machine into the rooms. "The court ruled that you can review documents, and take notes if you wish," he told us, "But you have no right to make copies of this private property." He was quite conclusive, like he had been instructed about this possibility, in no uncertain terms, by his bosses. The delivery person left, but we persuaded him that since we had already made our first monthly payment, he should not take his copy machine with him just yet. He left it in the hall. Well then. Back to court we went.

This time, Ken and Bruce and I still sat at one council table, but NSP and Westinghouse, having been joined by INPO and EPRI during our previous Court adventure, were now also joined by Framatome, the French nuclear steam generator fabricator, and Babcock & Wilcox, the Canadian fabricator, and Siemens, the German fabricator. The Nuclear Regulatory Commission was also snooting around. In other words, Ken and Bruce and I, with our small army, had arrayed against us every provider of pressurized water nuclear reactors in the world, along with their governmental regulators and major trade and research associations.

They were all there because failing Westinghouse equipment had created a multibillion-dollar open market in the US for steam generators, and all these outfits had proprietary and classified information on the record. If you're wondering, it was Case No. CIV-4-93-680. As Eric G. Dahlin from Cambridge, Ontario testified in an Affidavit dated May 4, 1995 on behalf of Babcock & Wilcox Industries, Ltd., they were all there because, "B&W is extremely disturbed by the attempt of the Prairie Island Coalition Against Nuclear Storage to obtain from Northern States Power the information provided by B&W to NSP in conjunction with B&W's bid to supply replacement nuclear steam generators to NSP."

The litigants, still itching to snarl at each other, had instead to settle for snarling at Ken and Bruce and myself while INPO, EPRI and the rest of the pertinent nuclear industry babysat their table. Ken made the argument that if the discovery rights His Honor had bestowed upon us were not just some hollow gesture, the information we discovered needed to have credibility in the eyes of the public. To be credible, we needed to be able to document our documents, so to speak. We needed to be able to produce copies of documents that we discovered, not just notes of documents that could be easily dismissed and discounted. We needed authentic copies of the original actual documents. NSP and Westinghouse argued that proprietary information was involved, and surely, while the Prairie Island Coalition Against Nuclear Storage may have been given the right to review certain documents in this proceeding as a matter of public interest, it did not follow that the Prairie Island Coalition Against Nuclear Storage had a right to violate the confidentiality of litigants as they exchanged private, privileged, and proprietary information while they negotiated with each other over how many hundreds of millions of dollars Westinghouse would have to pay.

Maybe, though, they should have thought more about the value of their private proprietary information before they resorted to a public forum to resolve their private differences, because the judge essentially agreed with Ken. Judge Rosenbaum ruled that if a document we reviewed contained information that we deemed the public had an interest in knowing, we had a right to a copy of that document. Unfortunately, he did not rule that *we* had the right to make the copies ourselves, but even so, we got to wheel our copy machine into NSP's rooms up in the 1st Bank Building while the NSP guard duty guy silently fumed as he watched us set up shop.

After some haggling, the deal was that we would review documents, decide if they warranted copying, and if so, indicate on the form Bruce had designed. Then, at the end of each day, we would submit all the forms our discovery team had filled out to the NSP guard duty guy, complete with identification of the Bates numbered pages of which we wanted copies, and the guard duty guy would make copies on paper we procured, of the Bates identified pages we specified, and give them to us first thing the following business day. Okay then. Our small army went back to work.

On the second day following this deal, we were shocked – SHOCKED - I tell you, to find great disparity between what we had asked for in terms of copies, and the copies the NSP guard duty guy was actually providing. The reason we knew there was a disparity was because, as per Bruce's instructions, we filled out *two* forms for each copy request. One we handed to the NSP guard duty guy. The other, we gave to Bruce. The next morning, after the guard duty guy plopped down the copies he had made for us on Bruce's table, Bruce reviewed the Bates Numbers of the pages in the plopped down pile and compared them with the Bates Numbers on the copies of the request forms that Bruce had kept. They were not the same. We did not even bother with the NSP guard duty guy.

Back to Court we went.

As Ken and Bruce and I sat waiting at our table in US Federal District Court for the requisite "Hear Ye Hear Ye," it was quite noticeable that at the table next door all the suits from NSP, Westinghouse, Electric Power Research Institute, Institute for Nuclear Power Operators, Siemens, Framatome, Babcock & Wilcox, and the Nuclear Regulatory Commission seemed anxious. As Judge Rosenbaum strode into his courtroom with all the attendant clamor, it became apparent as to why. The judge was not pleased.

After the preliminaries, the judge just cut to the chase. "If they ask for it," he snapped, "then you shall produce it. Furthermore," he continued, "Litigants (meaning NSP and Westinghouse) shall compensate Petitioners (meaning us) $50,000 in this instance of wrongful behavior and an additional $50,000 for every subsequent instance of wrongful behavior that comes before this court." As court adjourned, I sneered smugly at the NSP suit while holding out my hand, palm up for the money. But Ken told me to behave myself, so I had to be content with my sneer as we left and went back to work.

After that, things went fairly smoothly. Every morning, five or six of our foot soldiers showed up and worked the morning with Bruce, and those who had to leave at noon had reinforcements to replace them until quitting time. I helped out well over half the time. We got very proficient at sorting out information that was helpful, and skimming past chaff that was not. Copies of pages we requested were produced without further ado, and the NSP guard duty guy was polite and helpful as we reviewed box after box. This went on for months.

We learned about and documented the details of steam generator tube pits that were buried in sludge piles abutting tubes where the tubes connected to the tubesheet at the bottom of steam generators, where the 3,242 tubes are connected to the pipes that deliver pressurized, super-heated water to and from the reactor core. We learned about intergranular attack and stress corrosion cracking in the tubesheet crevice region; about dented intersections with axial and circumferential cracking at support plates; apex cracks and tangent cracks in U-bends; tube support plate thinning, or wastage; fretting wear at antivibration bars; primary water stress corrosion cracking.

We learned about how NSP inspected steam generator tubes with Rotating Coil Probes, each probe containing three different coils: a 0.115-inch pancake coil; a 0.080-inch pancake coil for discrimination of inside versus outside diameter signals; and the Plus + Point coils. These probes emit an electrical signal as they traverse their tubes, and cracks, pinholes, and pitting in a tube trigger eddy currents in the electrical signal that describe the dimensions of pits and pinholes, the depth and length of tube cracks, and whether they are axial, running the length of the tube, or circumferential. This probe was also used, the documents said, to resolve distorted signals caused by bobbin probe eddy current inspections, and we believed the documents to be truthful.

We learned about remedial actions NSP took. It reduced operating temperature, which slowed, but did not eliminate the several types of tube cracking. It messed around with water chemistry in a variety of ways. It elevated hydrazine levels and reduced acidic conditions due to free sodium hydroxide formation in the crevice regions through molar ration control to maintain the cation to anion ratio (sodium to chloride) at less than one. NSP flushed crevices with boric acid, and then decided to add boric acid online, although the effectiveness of this remedial action was controversial within the industry. It tried a bunch of other chemical inhibitors that centered around titanium compounds. It reduced the probability of tube leak outages with preventive tube sleeving, whereby a smaller tube gets welded inside the original tube. But then, after sleeving, NSP could not follow degradation mechanisms, and lost ability to examine tube support plate intersections above the sleeve. And besides, sleeved tubes soon leaked, anyway. NSP elevated its inspection protocol in terms of frequency, number and length of tubes inspected, and probe sophistication. It escalated its maintenance program, and still tube defects were mounting and causing all steam generators to leak all the time.

One document we uncovered originated with Gerald H. Neils, Executive Engineer, Nuclear Generation, Northern States Power Co. He wrote in a letter to John Taylor of the Electric Power Research Institute on January 7, 1991, (Discovery Document Numbers 06053101 – 06053103, paragraph 3) "So, if we are stuck on Inconel and stuck with crevices, then it is virtually a given that we will end up with steam generators that are no better than *almost* good enough." (Emphasis in the original.) This quotation inspired the title of a twenty-five minute video the Prairie Island Coalition Against Nuclear Storage produced in 1997 entitled, *Good Nukes – Almost Good Enough.* This video, which includes details about how a nuclear steam generator catastrophe unfolds, is documented with some thirteen authoritative reference sources and forty-two footnotes. We distributed it to numerous media outlets, state officials and school districts throughout Minnesota and Wisconsin that would be impacted if such an event were to occur at Prairie Island. A few copies are still available, but they are very expensive, and you need the right equipment to play it.

Not everything we reviewed had to do with the scientific examination of the multifaceted physical characteristics of steam generator tube degeneration, inspecting steam generator tube degeneration, remedial action to reduce steam generator tube degeneration, and internal as well as external politics to manage steam generator tube degeneration. There were also juicy tidbits. One of my favorites had to do with the passwords some NSP engineer chose to use so he could participate in electronic discussions EPRI was conducting about steam generator tube degeneration. After this guy typed in, "For all things living, great and small." he was good to go. On one hand, I already knew it. On the other, despite the overwhelming commitment, at least superficially, to science and rational examination of physical reality evidenced by all these Bates-numbered documents, it was stunning to witness this innocent acknowledgment of a mindset firmly fixated in a tawdry belief system that directly elevated greed, power and money for themselves over public health and safety. And belief, as we all know, is a low level of consciousness.

In all, we reviewed well over a million pages of documents, and secured copies of more than 60,000 pages. These pages led us to a detailed understanding of an absolutely horrific set of circumstances that the nuclear industry and its regulators were toying with as they all haggled over their money. By early 1996, almost 600 tubes in the four Prairie Island steam generators had been plugged. Without plugging, each of these tubes could have ruptured. Virtually all of the rest of them were degraded to one level or another, and a large number of those were leaking. As the days passed, our awareness grew of the mounting threat of a cascading, simultaneous, multiple tube rupture event in each of the 60+ pressurized water reactors owned by US utilities who had not yet swapped out Westinghouse steam generators that were deteriorating at an accelerating rate.

We became increasingly alarmed. Toward the end of February 1996, we knew in detail how this event would unfold. It would begin when a degraded tube, any one of the seven or eight hundred thousand of them in steam generators around the country, but probably one with a circumferential crack, would rupture. Then, a jet of super high-pressure 600°F water would pound a hammer shock on surrounding tubes while that water simultaneously exploded into steam because the pressure boundary was breached. These powerful new additional stresses would cause some, perhaps many of the surrounding tubes, themselves pitted, cracked and/or corroded, to also rupture. And then their adjacent tubes would rupture, and so forth. A cascading, multiple tube rupture event would be underway, with primary water forcing itself through the exploding steam generator into the secondary water loop. Steam-line pressure relief valves in the secondary water loop outside the containment vessel would open, and vent radioactive steam into the atmosphere.

As primary water hemorrhages into the secondary loop, water pressure on the massive volume of super-heated primary water in the reactor core will drop precipitously. This will cause the water in the core to violently boil. The resulting rapidly rising steam pressure inside the reactor core will force primary water out, and the core, no longer cooled by primary water, and with the emergency core cooling system overwhelmed, will rapidly rise in temperature, and melt. Molten fuel will collect at the bottom of the reactor vessel and melt down through the floor and into the ground beneath. This has been called the China Syndrome.

During the meltdown, molten fuel will burn through containment and contact groundwater under the plant. Resulting steam explosions will spread radioactive fuel particles and debris, according to atmospheric conditions at the time, and for a substantial period of time, for hundreds of miles downwind, thereby contaminating many thousands of square miles. A massive sacrifice zone, akin to that surrounding the Chernobyl reactors, will be created and require evacuation and abandonment past the foreseeable future. That is what Judge Rosenbaum enabled us to discover. In due course, as at Chernobyl, teams of riflemen wearing protective clothing would be sent into the zone to shoot the starving pets. What the shtup!

Now that we know this, how do we sound the alarm? If we do it as publicly as possible, who will believe us? Should we quietly inform a selected handful of responsible public officials? How about we select a group of the most strategic elected officials we can muster, arm them with our discovery documents, and turn them loose? This discussion lasted maybe half a day.

For better and for worse, obviously, the nuclear suits were keeping track of our progress. When we knew we had the goods, we stopped showing up for discovery at the 1st Bank Building and set about organizing our response. But when we stopped showing up, they knew they were busted. They knew we had the goods. They moved quickly.

On March 4, 1996, as we were preparing our packet of irrefutably incriminating evidence, identifying our team of courageous public officials (Senator Paul David Wellstone was still among the living), and informing them of the task we were desperate to help them accomplish, *Inside NRC,* an exclusive report of the U.S. Nuclear Regulatory Commission, came out with Vol. 18, No.5. For the first time, there was public disclosure by the nuclear industry of the magnitude of the problem.

In significant part, here is what it said under the following headline:

JACKSON PRODS STAFF TO EXPEDITE STEAM GENERATOR RULES AS CRACKING SURGES

NRC Chair Shirley Jackson is pushing the staff to develop a steam generator rule quickly, as the number – and kinds – of cracks being found in steam generator tubes in U.S. nuclear power plants increases dramatically.

Executive Director for Operations James Taylor told the commission the staff has made "substantial progress" on the generic rulemaking effort underway, but he could not yet commit to a timeline because there are so many outstanding technical issues to be studied and resolved. "Unfortunately, new forms of degradation are appearing," Taylor said at a commission meeting February 7. "I believe this is one of the most serious challenges facing the industry today."

Recent inspections at PWRs have turned up "many more cracking indications than were anticipated," Office of Nuclear Reactor Regulations (NRR) Director Bill Russell told the commission. The number of cracking indications in steam generator tubes at a given plant commonly "will jump from the tens in one outage, to the hundreds – or thousands – in the next outage," he said.

The staff is developing a "risk-informed, performance-based rule" to address what it terms "numerous shortcomings with the current regulatory framework." Russell said the rule would establish criteria and inspection techniques, as well as lay out how vendors could qualify their inspection techniques.

The staff said it would try to get a paper ready for the commission in May laying out a schedule for the rulemaking effort. Because of the unexpected surge in the number of cracks being found, "putting out fires" and conducting "case-by-case reviews" of steam generator tube inspections have been taking up a lot of the staff time, Russell added.

Loss of steam generator tube integrity has serious safety implications because the thousands of tubes form a significant portion of the reactor coolant pressure boundary, Ashok Thadani, associate director of NRR, said. There have been nine tube ruptures at U.S. plants to date. In each case, "the consequences have been minimal, and there have never been multiple tube ruptures," he said.

NRC staffers are studying conditions and scenarios which they believe could pose the greatest health risk to the public. "If a severe accident produces conditions under which degraded tubes can fail, significant radiological releases may occur," the staff said. Accident scenarios of greatest concern are those that involve high temperature and pressure in the system, where tube integrity could be lost.

"We've done many years of research on how the containment would behave" under those conditions, Thadani noted. "While we have confidence in the containment, we don't have that same confidence in how steam generator tubes would behave….It's clear to us we have to capture the new degradation mechanisms."

This uncharacteristically candid, public, and straightforward acknowledgment by the industry of the problem threw our plans regarding public disclosure of our discovery information into disarray. The industry was now embarked upon, and publicly committed to the remedial action we were poised to advocate. And in fact, steam generator rules were promulgated expeditiously, and decrepit steam generators started getting swapped out quickly, without the litigious haggling. The timing of their remediation actions, however, leads directly to a conclusion that if we had not first nailed them dead to rights, it is quite likely, if not probable, that corrective action would have continued to languish. Arguably, without our intervention, the industry's corrective action would have been a reaction to an occurrence. But we did bust them, they did respond. So far, at least, we have yet to experience a simultaneous multiple tube rupture event at a pressurized water reactor. Knock on wood. As John Hodgeman says, "You're welcome."

Unfortunately, we never were able to collect the $50,000 fine imposed by Judge Rosenbaum, and despite repeated efforts, we were also unable to secure a copy of the NSP/Westinghouse Settlement Agreement. This case, like all the others, never went to trial.

All this occurred almost twenty years ago. After twenty years, the first generation of steam generators was on the brink of catastrophic failure. Maybe somebody should call up the NRC to check in on how the second generation is doing.

Many years later, on January 5, 2012, at the infamous Earl Brown Center on the St. Paul Campus of the University of Minnesota, NAWO's Environmental Justice Coordinator Lea Foushee got a scholarship to attend a "State of the Plate" conference sponsored by Blue Cross Blue Shield of Minnesota and a couple other organizations. Also attending was an older gentleman who happened to pair himself up with Lea as they sat next to each other in the auditorium during the "Hi How Are You" exercise designed to get to know your fellow conference attendees. This gentleman asked Lea to kindly go first in introducing herself, which she did. He was so intrigued by Lea's origins and impressive history that he encouraged her to expound further on her work with the North American Water Office until the time-period for this exercise was almost up, at which point Lea politely inquired, "Well then. What about you?"

So the kindly gentleman told Lea why he was at this "State of the Plate" conference in St. Paul, and offered that he had formerly worked with Westinghouse.

At this point, Lea quite vociferously exclaimed, "Oh Ho! Westinghouse, is it? Cascading simultaneous multiple steam generator tube ruptures!!! We're the ones who busted your ass!!"

"It wasn't me! It wasn't me!" protested the gentleman. "I wasn't even in the nuclear division!" Thing is, he knew exactly to that which

Lea had referred, and it got him so flustered and disturbed that he sprang from his seat and fled the auditorium as fast as his legs would carry him, to never be seen again.

Additional evidence of the socially deviant nature of nuclear power's managers, as if we did not have enough, is provided by the ongoing drama circulating around the Monticello nuclear plant, also owned and operated by Xcel Energy, and located on the Mississippi River about ten miles upstream from the primary water intake for the City of Minneapolis. Monticello is a single unit boiling water reactor made by General Electric and is one of the three oldest operating reactors in the country. It is identical to the nuclear plants that exploded in Fukushima in March of 2011.

Apparently, this event began sometime well prior to November 2022 when NSP first noticed that something was awry and reported to the Nuclear Regulatory Commission (NRC) that radioactivity had been found in groundwater from an on-site monitoring well. Xcel reported that tritium concentrations in its groundwater sample were at five million picocuries per liter, which is among the highest concentrations ever reported from a leak at a reactor site. It should be noted that there is no known way to remove tritium, which is radioactive hydrogen, from water once it has been contaminated. As our friends at The Progressive Foundation published in their *NUKEWATCH QUARTERLY* for Spring 2024 (ISSN 1942-6305), the radioactivity contained in this leaked, tritiated water registered eight curies of radiation released to the environment. For comparison, when Three Mile Island went klaphlouie in 1979, the radioactivity it released, primarily iodine[131], amounted to fourteen curies. (The Progressive Foundation, a non-profit organization out of Luck, Wisconsin since 1980, shines light on nefarious activities of both civilian and military nuclear institutions and deserves your support.)

But Xcel Energy and the Minnesota Department of Health did not bother to inform the public of the leak, around 400,000 gallons, they said, until four months later, in mid-March of 2023. The reason for the delay is that when springtime came around, it would be time to shut the plant down anyway for refueling. By holding out during that four-month period, Xcel Energy's incoming revenue from the plant was something north of $160,000,000 more than it would have been had it shut down when it first discovered radioactivity in its monitoring well. Then, on March 18, 2023, it announced with much fanfare that the contamination had not reached the Mississippi River and that there was no risk to the public. Then, a few days later, Xcel Energy announced a second leak of several hundred gallons of contaminated water because the tank into which contaminated water was being collected had overflowed. Not bad, for a clown show.

So. Every year, the NRC holds a public annual meeting for every nuclear power plant in the country at a community center in the municipality that hosts the power plant. At Monticello's annual meeting on May 25, 2023, we learned that the leak occurred because Control Rod Drive pipes in between the Condenser Building and the Reactor Building, required to properly manage the pressure and flow of primary water circulating through the core, had corroded so that they acted more like a coffee filter than essential plumbing at a nuclear power plant. The two pipes corroded, evidently, because when NSP build the plant in the late 1960s, the construction team did not think to put a roof over the space between the two buildings. Over the course of fifty-two years or so, with storm water wetness corroding on the outside and water under pressure on the inside, it was just too much. At some point, primary water started oozing out, undetected, until it showed up in a monitoring well. The March 18, 2023, announcement was forced by the fact that Xcel realized at that point that heavy equipment needed to get brought in to deal with the leakage, and neighbors would start to talk if they saw heavy equipment showing up.

By May 10, 2023, it was clear that tritium was not the only radioactive contaminant in the leakage. Analysis submitted by Xcel Energy to the NRC on that date confirmed that iodine[131], iodine[133], iodine[135], xenon[133] and xenon[135] were also present. Then, on December 18, 2023, Xcel Energy reported that it really wasn't 400,000 gallons that had leaked into the ground, but rather more like an estimated 829,000 gallons, and it acknowledged that the released radioactivity was therefore more like fourteen curies, which is about as much as was released at Three Mile Island in 1979.

Xcel acknowledged on July 20, 2023, that a little bit of the contaminated water may have reached the Mississippi River, but it is demonstrating that deeds sometimes speak louder than words because by August, it was working to install a steel groundwater barrier wall 600 feet long and forty feet deep in an effort to segregate the leakage from the river. The efficacy of this structure will be tested for the next 120 years or so, as Minneapolis continues extracting about fifty-seven million gallons of drinking water per day about ten miles downstream. Meanwhile, in January 2023, before publicly acknowledging the leak, Xcel applied to the NRC for another extension of its operating license so it can operate until it turns eighty.

In any event, without totally deranged economics, there is no future for commercial nuclear power. It's much too expensive. This was the conclusion of a study published in the Proceedings of the National Academy of Sciences in July 2018. The authors of the report had been enthusiastically supportive of nuclear power and viewed its loss as an option for producing electricity as a matter of "profound concern." But the fact remains that it is much too expensive. As noted earlier, the only new reactors to come online in the past thirty years are Vogtle Units 3 & 4 in Georgia. They cost over $13.5 million per installed megawatt, while new solar costs about $1 million per installed megawatt, and new wind comes in around $2 million per installed megawatt.

Finally, it should be clear that commercial nuclear technology is terribly unforgiving. The potential for major radioactive releases due to human error can be minimized, but not eliminated. The potential for major radioactive releases due to component failure will continue to increase as reactors age, as critical parts corrode or become embrittled due to neutron bombardment, and except for Vogtle 3 & 4, the aging process is well underway. Accidents happen. Like at Three Mile Island and Chernobyl. Or natural disasters, like at Fukushima in 2011. The only clean nuclear power is fusion power, the process that powers the stars. Not Taylor Swift, but like our sun and the lights in the nighttime sky. Major advances here on Earth are being made in fusion technology, and the time may come when fusion reactors are commercially viable and finally fulfill the promise of nuclear power being "too cheap to meter." But that time is not now.

# Chapter 7

## What Does CLEAR Energy Management Look Like?

The technology part of the energy transition is unfolding as it usually does when humans figure out a new advancement, given enough time. If it were not for Climate Chaos and warring and messy, disrespectful mining of copper, lithium, and other metals required by the energy transition, our celebration of the glorious and triumphant victory of renewable energy and energy storage technologies over central station technology could be more joyful. But even here, in the heart of North America, where Talon Metals tracked down a very rich nickel, copper, cobalt vein near Tamarack, in Aitkin County, Minnesota, and teamed up with Rio Tinto for the extraction, the miners think their sulfate contaminated waste water is okay to dump into our surface waters if they just dilute it to some arbitrary standard that is not protective of sensitive resources, like Manomin, wild rice. Cleaning up the mining industry may turn out to be more than just cosmetic, one could hope, but just what is the cost of pollution, and what do you think the payment options are?

Continued warring threatens to make the question moot, and when younger people take action to protest the warring, the adults send in the cops to arrest the kids. How hopeful is that?

For now, however, the glorious and triumphant victory of renewable energy and energy storage technologies is a victory for people who want their energy services delivered cleanly. Well, cleaner, anyway. The modern technologies present magnificent opportunities for those who also want their energy services delivered with some sense of local ownership, some sense that communities, urban to rural, that host renewable energy projects, are not just bit players in an extraction program that mostly benefits others who live far away and participate primarily by getting paid lots of money for the use of lots of their money. At long last, the time approaches when the appeasement of Electric Utility Oligarchs and their corporate cartel will no longer be a prerequisite for getting electric utility services. Certainly, the energy technologies of the Modern Era cost much less to install and operate than the central station technologies they are replacing, and their ability to be deployed and intelligently connected in large numbers, in a dispersed and distributed manner, relatively close to the loads they serve, elevates the security and reliability provided by the modern technologies way above standards that get applied in the Central Station Era.

Those things that remain in the way of society beginning to realize its CLEAR energy future are entirely human fabrications. Mostly, what is in the way is privilege that comes from wealth. Much of that wealth is "earned" through passive income and other blunt tax and investment perks designed to protect and accumulate wealth. Intermingle this accumulated wealth with ill-gotten gains produced by flawed incentives and monopoly protections, and you have your American version of oligarchs who manage their privilege to enhance the capital formations that dominate the electric utility industry, of which collectively, they own the major fraction of about seventy-two percent. The fact that most of the remaining fraction of this wealth is tied up in various sorts of retirement plans does not change the reality that most electric utility management decisions, even now in the twilight of the Central Station Era, are designed to protect and enhance the wealth produced by central station machines. For example, as late as April 25, 2024, an EPA rule gives about 200 US coal plants until 2039 - 2039!! - to sequester their carbon emissions. The thing of it is, though, all the regulatory and financial instruments that produce this wealth are all human constructs, and polite society, such as it is, can change human constructs through democratic processes, hopefully, and do so in a timeframe that still matters.

Such change will not happen unless and until a large enough segment of the energy consuming population understands with some precision what it is they want, and then organize themselves socially, economically and politically to get it. That includes mustering enough political power to properly eliminate the monopoly power structures that presently dominate the electric utility landscape. When central station oligarchs get stripped of their monopoly powers, a pathway leading to economic democracy will have been opened, and common sense organizing and educating will guide us toward it.

So, what do we want?

Recognizing that there are a variety of management and ownership structures that would enable CLEAR energy services to get delivered, what might a CLEAR energy system look like beyond the vague outline of an acronym? We will try to fill in that outline a bit, but one thing is certain: if polite society survives, it will have learned to understand and practice the full measure and meaning of "energy democracy," and if we can accomplish energy democracy, we will find that economic democracy will also be within reach.

At one level, the management and ownership structures of the Modern Era are likely to be somewhat similar to existing municipal power structures, or electric cooperatives, or how the good citizens of the Great State of Nebraska organize virtually their entire state into public power districts. Managers and directors of these energy service providers are accountable not to shareholders intent on maximizing their own private profit, but rather, to their municipal residents, their coop members, and in the case of Nebraska, a Board of Directors is elected from within each of twenty-five chartered territories which include all or parts of eighty-four of Nebraska's ninety-three counties, fifty-two cities and villages and about eighty communities. The Nebraska Public Power District Boards are accountable to the constituents who elect them. Not that Nebraska is ahead of the curve in terms of deploying the modern technologies, because it isn't. But it has an energy management *structure* that is capable of responding quickly, and without interference from energy oligarchs, as soon as its constituent base gets informed and activated enough to expedite the transition.

A big difference, however, will be how service territories get defined. In significant part, service territories will be defined electrically, as opposed to geographically, power company by power company. In the Modern Era, energy consumers will become familiar with the concept of "energy neighborhoods."

Think about what could happen when the concept of municipal power company management gets applied within the footprint of every load-serving substation in a state and nation. Each load-serving substation would provide power to its own discrete, intelligently controlled microgrid that would enable all loads within its footprint to be managed in a most efficient and coordinated manner, and each of these microgrids would be interconnected with all its neighboring substation microgrids for security and reliability purposes. A network, so to speak. Within each footprint of our interconnected network, there is an opportunity for local ownership of the generation infrastructure that serves the footprint.

On the supply side, as noted in Chapter 5, new electrical generation and storage capacity can be strategically sized and connected so that all the power will be consumed within the substation footprint, and none of it will ever flow back up to the higher voltage system. This new capacity can be brought online as soon as it gets installed with no need for *any* transmission enhancements. So, for example, let's assume that a community of about 6,000 homes and a bunch of small businesses and light industry is served by a fifteen MW substation that has a minimum load within its footprint at night when everyone's asleep, of five MW. Let's also assume that the people living and working within this footprint operate their own "municipal power" type structure that enables them, as a community and as individuals, to be as actively involved as they desire with the management and ownership of the electric utility infrastructure within their substation footprint. They are involved because their involvement directly serves their individual and collective financial and social interests, just like school boards and county commissioners.

Because its minimum load is five MW, the management of our substation-footprint "municipality" can therefore develop and deploy five megawatts of electrical generation and storage capacity and connect it to the low voltage side of their substation transformer, without ever causing problems on the higher voltage transmission system to which it is connected. All the power supplied on the low voltage side will follow a path of least electrical resistance to loads within the substation's footprint. None of it will ever get stepped up by the transformer for transmission on the higher voltage system. Incoming power from the grid will provide all energy requirements within the footprint that are above this minimum until our substation-footprint "municipality" decides to take its next step. Then, it will undertake a transmission analysis to identify costs to incrementally upgrade the higher voltage transmission system to which it is connected so that it can develop additional renewable electric generation capacity, some of which from time to time will flow back up to the higher voltage system. We'll get to that.

But for now, let's assume that the cost to develop the five MW generation and storage facility is $1 million for one MW of solar capacity, $8 million for four MW of wind capacity, and $3 million for one MW of storage capacity for ten hours, for a total cost of $12 million. Let's further assume that this new generation and storage capacity is sufficient to provide an average continuous power flow of 3.5 MW into the footprint of the substation, and that the retail value paid by consumers within the substation footprint for electricity flowing into their footprint from the higher voltage system is $0.10/kWh. With these assumptions, our "substation municipality" will manage an annual revenue stream of $3,066,000. (3,500 kW x 8760 hrs./yr. x $0.10/kWh =

$3,066,000) Consumer members of our "substation municipality" will pay their monthly electric bills to their own "substation municipality," which will retain the value of the electricity produced by its five MW project, and forward the remainder to the remnant of the Central Station Era that is still operating the higher voltage grid and the generators that provide power to it, for the few remaining years until it is bought out and replaced by an aggregation of "substation municipalities."

Our "substation municipality" will manage its initial annual budget of $3+ million to compensate its very modest management and maintenance work force, and in the early years, devote much of the rest of it toward paying down capital costs of the five MW installation and preparing for the next increment of infrastructure development. As long as we're assuming the enlightened behavior that overcame the monopolistic behavior of the fading Central Station Era, hence the existence of our "substation municipality," let's also assume that governmental entities have avoided the more fascistic bends and are trending closer to a democracy guided by the common sense required to navigate the atmospheric circumstances that will continue to become more eventful. If things go the other way, the rest of it will not much matter. We can therefore also assume constructive state and federal fiscal policy that enables the "substation municipality" to pay off the loans it used to purchase and install its five MW facility in a relatively short time, perhaps under ten years, while balancing the need to ramp up demand side efficiency improvement programs.

Once the debt on the five MW system is retired, revenue produced by the system can be managed to reduce energy bills for consumers within the substation footprint, to pay dividends to those consumers, to finance demand side programs that increase energy efficiency within the footprint, to support community well-being with enhancements for parks and libraries and community theater, or all of the above.

Now let's say that toward the end of the seven to ten year payback period, our "substation municipality" coordinated with its pertinent interconnected neighboring "substation municipalities" to conduct the transmission power flow analysis required to deploy the next increment of strategically sized and located generation. With the foundational knowledge this power flow analysis provides, the networked, interconnected "substation municipalities" now flourishing across the region will identify and prioritize thousands of locations for new generation, with storage where appropriate, and strategically size projects so that the electricity they produce will be accommodated by the newly enhanced higher voltage transmission system. These efforts will be financed with revenue no longer siphoned off by oligarchs, but that instead is retained by the owner/members of the "substation municipalities." Then they will conduct another power flow analysis. This iterative process will continue adding new generation that is sized and located according to the results of transmission power flow analysis until the interconnected grid is saturated with strategically sized and sited dispersed and distributed renewable generation and storage systems, and in the process, incrementally back out the remainder of the central station fleet except for all but the densest of industrial loads, like mining and processing metals with environmentally respectful practices.

The above hyper-hypothetical is one simplistic example from a more rural type of setting. Defining an electrical neighborhood in a more urban setting is less clear-cut because multiple substations play a role in delivering electric services to any given address, but that just means people living in urban settings have the opportunity to determine their own way of defining their electrical neighborhoods, and what the optimal size of such a neighborhood actually is. Whether any given address in a region served by multiple substations is in one neighborhood or another does not really matter so long as energy neighborhoods get defined, and the entire urban landscape is covered. Another difference from a rural setting is that solar generation will be much more dominant, while wind generation has more constraints.

So, let's suppose that after analyzing urban substation locations and power flows from those substations into urban neighborhoods, discrete, comprehensive, interconnected electrical neighborhoods are identified. Each discrete energy neighborhood then forms its own "substation municipality." Certain functions, like managing electric bills, could be consolidated. But each urban "substation municipality" would inventory its energy neighborhood for candidate solar development and energy storage sites, and proceed to deploy that capacity, substation by substation, up to the lowest load limit. Then another power flow analysis, and then another increment of electrical capacity installations can proceed.

When such an energy development strategy receives priority policy status and effective financing, *i.e.*, iterations of power flow analysis followed by transmission enhancements followed by strategic deployment of new generation capacity, and then another iterative cycle, it will complete the supply-side energy transition in relatively short order.

Just as the optimum set of ownership structures for operating interconnected, substation-based microgrid networks has yet to be determined for the supply side, so too, the optimum set of rate designs to reward power companies for energy efficient management, rather than energy consumption, remains a work in progress. But a good place to start improving forthwith would be to dramatically expand existing IOU Conservation Improvement Programs (CIP). For example, Xcel Energy's NSP Division is required to spend two percent of its revenue on conservation programs, and its 2023 revenue was $6.48 billion, so, a little over $97 million for conservation, and we have discussed the effectiveness of this expenditure relative to the technical potential to increase end use energy efficiency. But what if NSP, or whomever, did their conservation stuff as usual, but also did "direct installation programs?"

Direct Installation programs are programs in which a utility hires contractors who go block by block, and house by house throughout a community to inventory end use functions and the devices used to perform those functions. Obviously, anyone who objects can opt out, but then, guided by this inventory, each house or business, block by block, gets specific information about all the energy efficiency improvements that could reasonably be undertaken at that specific address. Then, the homeowner or business proprietor would have a discussion with the utility's Direct Installation contractor, and together, they decide which of the specified and ranked energy efficiency improvements is of interest to the homeowner or proprietor. Then Inclusive Financing kicks in, the upgrades are made, and the homeowner or proprietor pays for the upgrades over time with part of the savings on the monthly energy bill made possible by the energy efficiency improvements. The other part of the value of the energy saved rewards the homeowner or proprietor for making the investment.

If a sense of urgency were to overtake society as Climate Chaos accelerates, Direct Installation Programs easily lend themselves to ramping up so that more dwellings and establishments get their upgrade sooner rather than later. All that would be required for this to occur, would be to nick a bit of the Electric Utility Oligarchs' return-on-investment and, for example, up NSP's 2 percent to, say, ten percent or twenty percent or forty percent, depending on society's assessment of the accelerating destruction. This, in turn, would spur the maturation of a comprehensive recycling industry, as well as create innumerable good-paying jobs and technology innovations that would accompany a large-scale swap-out of old appliances of all sorts, for new, efficient ones.

Such a move, obviously, would produce a major financial hit on the incumbent IOU capital formations, but similar hits happen all the time in free and fair market economies that are driven by actual market forces, particularly when paradigms shift. If the Electric Utility Oligarchs do not like it, they can easily find another home, in our free and fair market economy, for their accumulated wealth. In addition, however, a dramatic increase in required CIP expenditures is extremely fitting and proper because much, if not most, of the private wealth produced by the electric utility industry is the result of society's failure to incorporate "externalized costs" that have been attached to the production of electric utility services throughout the Central Station Era. Upping CIP requirements is a simple and straightforward process for "clawing back" a portion of ill-gotten gains procured at the expense of our environment.

Already, these externalized costs are causing enough destruction so that insurance companies in California and Florida, for example, are raising rates so dramatically to cover storm, flood and fire events that many people can no longer afford insurance. In some instances already, insurance coverage is no longer even available. Areas in which these types of costs and constraints are being experienced are getting larger and are found in more locations. So, what is the cost of Climate Chaos induced drought and famine around the world? Or of managing the destruction caused in coastal cities around the world by rising sea levels due to expanding oceans and melting glaciers as our atmospheric blanket traps more heat? Certainly, in a democratic country powered by free and fair market forces, it is appropriate to attach a portion of the cost of this destruction and essential mitigation to those who profit from the operation of the machines that are responsible for the threat and the destruction. A dramatic increase of required CIP expenditures is an easy to understand, common sense adjustment to electric utility rate design that would catalyze the deployment of technologies and management practices capable of addressing this crisis that defines our time here on Earth.

Humans can certainly complete the energy transition, given enough time. How much time? How fast must the transition to a CLEAR energy future happen if it is to help reverse the trend of slowing ocean currents that threaten to collapse sometime early next month? Or next year, maybe? Time will tell, as the energy transition is more of a process than an event, and all the warring stunts the process and makes it much more sluggish no matter how you look at it.

For humans to complete a transition to CLEAR energy, slowing ocean currents or not, bullies must be stopped along the way, and fascists must be kept from power. Bullies usually stop when their nose starts to bleed, and fascists need a jail, and that, sometimes, is where the warring comes in. But time is of the essence, and from a Climate

Chaos mitigation perspective, warring is utterly antithetical. Warring requires a whole lot of metal stuff that uses lots of dirty fuel to fabricate, and then it gets blown up so it will either sit and rust, or get recycled, using lots more dirty fuel, into something else that gets blown up. The gasses released when things blow up, and all the fires of war add insult to injury. Then there's methane pipelines that get destroyed, releasing bulk quantities of this potent greenhouse gas into the atmosphere, to say nothing of all the wealth that gets diverted to pay for it all. No matter what, warring dramatically accelerates our plunge into Climate Chaos. Bullies must be stopped, and fascists need to go to jail, but at this point, for civilized society to have a chance, warring must be ended. The global community needs to figure out how to stop it. Perhaps a globalized mobilization of the courageous and heroic willing can be organized to insert themselves into war zones to stop the carnage and enforce negotiations. The United Nations isn't working, and the adults are busting kids who protest. But if the warring does not stop, an apocalyptic future awaits.

The thing of it is, though, energy management is the foundation upon which virtually all our social and physical structures stand. With proper energy management, issues surrounding food and housing and health care and entertainment of all sorts, and other requirements of the human condition can be satisfied. That is what proper energy management does. It solves problems. It eliminates motivations for war and the sense of deprivation and impotence that often leads to fascism. If the warring can be controlled, civilization as we know it will be able to divert the worst of Climate Chaos. Maybe. Who knows what happens when ocean currents stall out and the web of life gets rent by the forces causing Earth's seventh mass extinction event, which is now well underway. But if there is to be salvation, the modern technologies required for it are mature, readily available and extremely cost-effective, even more so if one counts the cost of the destruction that maybe we can avoid. The policies and programs required to manage those technologies so that our environment gets protected, social equity gets promoted, and that provide for local economic justice are within sight, even if these goals are still on civilization's horizon. We should be able to bring them into focus. Maybe, instead of falling off the proverbial cliff, humanity can at least guide its awkward slide down a steep ravine and figure out how to best manage things once we get to the bottom of it.

In every state of every nation on the planet, the hard work of securing a CLEAR energy future is underway. If you want to help to get it done in time, get involved. There's ample opportunity.

# Chapter 8

## Organize and Mobilize to Democratize Electricity

"In a democracy there are only two types of power:
there's organized people and organized money,
and organized money only wins when people
aren't organized."

–Benjamin Jealous

Put another way, organized people beat organized money every time the people are organized.

We have had a good look at how the electric utility system operates, and flaws within that operation, some of which are just deplorably disgusting, and others that may prove fatal to our continued ability to experience human civilization, such as it is. We have examined the evolution of the technologies that provide electric utility services, and the promise of modern technologies to deliver those services with a CLEAR intent. And we have described with an initial bit of specificity what a CLEAR electric utility system might look like. Now we will discuss what needs to happen in order to turn our CLEAR vision of electric utility management into a semblance of reality. It is time to get organized.

First things first: energy literacy must improve. It's hard to be organized when you do not know what's going on. That is where "powerful conversations" come in. As Minneapolis Energy Options and then Community Power engaged with Xcel Energy and Center-Point Energy over terms and conditions of their respective Franchise Agreements with the City of Minneapolis more than a decade ago, we understood that rallies and petition drives and other standard tools of community organizing were necessary, but nowhere near sufficient if we actually expected to improve energy management in Minneapolis. If we wanted to improve things over the long-term, we needed people in Minneapolis who were not just somewhat displeased at the pollution and the greedy extraction of wealth from their community, but who also had some understanding of how the extraction was orchestrated decade after decade by Xcel Energy and CenterPoint. Once people understand what is actually going on, we reasoned, along with the best of conspiracy theorists but bent differently, they will not put up with it anymore. If we were to make a difference, we needed activated citizens knowledgeable enough to challenge the status quo on the facts, and who are able to share information with their neighbors about the benefits city residents could be enjoying if energy were managed with CLEAR objectives.

Unfortunately, a good portion of the general population, when asked about where electricity comes from, will mostly point to a wall socket. So we created an electric utility curriculum called powerful conversations, designed specifically for our Upper Midwest region of the country, complete with literature and a map with visual aids to explain where energy resources are located, where power plants are located, the general principles regarding how the transmission system operates in the Central Station Era, how power flows through that system to energy consumers, and environmental, social and economic consequences attached to that flow of power. Then, the powerful conversations curriculum presents an overview of how the electric utility system could work with modern technologies phasing out the central station machines, and it facilitates a discussion about environmental and social justice benefits and local economic development opportunities that present themselves when energy gets managed correctly. This leads to the obvious discussions regarding what to do about this absurdly normal way we have of doing energy business.

We used our own social networks and names we gathered at rallies and petition drives to organize powerful conversations presentations. Powerful Conversations gets presented in peoples' homes with their neighbors invited, at community centers and churches, and wherever else an attentive audience can be attracted.

A public educational program such as powerful conversations that is geared to local circumstances fulfills an essential requirement of getting organized. Such a program can travel to county fairs and festivals and community celebrations and neighborhood groups of whatever sort, and it sets the stage for ongoing discussions that will mature into activities that need to happen in order to establish the relationships with bureaucrats, politicians, utility managers, media personnel and the general public that are required to accelerate the energy transition. In the process, it begins to establish the community, the nascent movement, if you will, that is becoming capable of carrying out necessary energy transition activities. Built into powerful conversations is a recognition that many aspects of the energy transition are shared in common around the country and around the world, but there are also aspects that apply uniquely to any given community.

With a movement that has as its foundation a cadre of activists whose knowledge of energy and energy management, gained through powerful conversations, prevents them from getting bamboozled by conventional utility business practices and management, the next step is to become familiar with decision-making proceedings regarding how energy services get delivered within your jurisdiction. These proceedings are usually conducted by state bureaucracies, and there is an unending stream of them. Energy utilities *always* need something. If it is not a rate-hike or a Certificate of Need for a new powerline or generation facility, it's a planning docket like Integrated Resource Planning, or a rule change required to accommodate some new set of circumstances created by the ongoing energy transition, or a pollution permit for some burner or system contributing to Climate Chaos, or a routing issue for some powerline. There is always something, and the job of this cadre of activists is to inventory dockets in all the pertinent bureaucracies, and prioritize them for purposes of intervention: what are the decisions being made by public utilities commissions, or pollution control agencies, or environmental quality boards, or health departments, and which of these decisions warrant public scrutiny with the intent of affecting the ultimate decision so that it better reflects CLEAR priorities, rather than the interests of energy oligarchs.

To do that, you need to know about the rules that govern administrative procedures. You do not need to necessarily *know* the rules, and you do not need to be a lawyer, and you do not need to have a lawyer. You just need to know where to find the rules so you can refer to them as needed. And if you know the rules well enough, you can initiate your own administrative proceeding. For example, the A-Squad at Community Power initiated our formal campaign for Inclusive Financing by rounding up support, including from the City of Minneapolis, environmental and social justice advocates, neighborhood groups, and spiritual communities doing their best to practice their values, and petitioned the Minnesota Public Utilities Commission to open a docket. Community Power took the lead. The proceeding did not turn out so good this first time through, but that is just because CenterPoint sabotaged the process when it finally figured out that we wouldn't let it turn Inclusive Financing into its own perverted profit center, and that instead, Inclusive Financing actually would improve end use efficiency, thereby reducing CenterPoint earnings. We'll do better next time when we again bring the issue forward. But the point is that when you're ready, you can initiate administrative proceedings, usually by petitioning the proper bureaucrats to open a docket regarding the change in rules governing electric utility management that you want to make. It's like being on offense, rather than just always playing defense.

But defense must be played, and it can be played well by picking the right set of dockets from the never-ending stream that flows through the bureaucracy. The primary criterion for deciding which dockets deserve intervention is how the decision will impact the on-going delivery of electric utility services, and how that impact has the potential to move us closer to, or further away from CLEAR energy services. The other primary criterion is whether you can muster the technical expertise to make your case, but that's mostly a matter of doing your homework. Also think about media messaging and how people can be mobilized to support the effort.

Once you have identified a docket worthy of your intervention, petition the administrator of the proceeding, usually an Administrative Law Judge (ALJ), to be included in the case. I have never been excluded from a proceeding in which I have petitioned for admittance. When your petition gets accepted, you're in. It's a lot of work. An overworked and properly motivated individual can manage participation in a docket, but having a team works better. Intervention involves studying the docket's foundational documents and applications, and the testimony of utility and state expert witnesses, and preparing yourself to cross-examine them. It involves preparing and presenting your own affirmed/sworn testimony and/or that of your own expert witnesses that you will present for cross-examination by other parties to the proceeding. It requires writing your own briefs and reply briefs and rebuttal briefs and surrebuttal briefs, and responding to the briefs and reply briefs and rebuttal briefs of all the other parties to the proceeding, and then preparing findings of fact and conclusions, and comments on the proposed findings of fact and conclusions of other parties, and then of the ALJ, and finally, arguing the case before the ultimate decision-making body.

Part of the strategy for determining where intervention is warranted involves the degree to which public participation can be organized. Virtually all dockets of whatever sort either have a physical hearing or two in which members of the general public can present their concerns for the record, or at a minimum, the proceeding will accept written comments from the public. That's the "inside game." But strategic interventions offer all sorts of opportunities for movement building, including petitions and rallies with leaflets and theater, and protest demonstrations.

The fundamental point: Clearly define objectives, step by step, toward a CLEAR energy future, and intervene strategically toward those objectives. Then activate the "outside game."

> The fundamental question: Who can enable you to get
> what you want?
> –Saul Alinsky

You need to clearly understand who that is for any given set of issues, and it is not usually utility executives. Well, they could, maybe, but they won't. Not unless forced by rule or law or shareholder resolution. Sometimes it is not the bureaucrats, either. Sometimes, it is the politicians. Then you have to go to the state legislature and make a bill become a law. Or stop a bad one. One of the laws that our A-Squad has its sights set on in Minnesota (in addition to CLEAR legislation) is the poison pill that blocks municipalities from forming municipals, the previously cited MN Stat. 216B.45. This law, designed in the heyday of the Central Station Era to protect investments into central station machines, stands squarely in the way of economic democracy and the social equity it will produce. This law must be amended or eliminated to create a clear and accessible pathway for municipalities to municipalize their energy utilities, and that involves politics, where there's different rules of process and procedure to figure out than with the bureaucrats. But either way, we need to enter decision-making arenas with enough substance and power to dramatically alter the trajectory of energy management.

Now we are talking Total Tactic. Total Tactic requires keen analysis to establish step-by-step objectives, and the venues in which those objectives can be realized. Total Tactic requires an informed and activated critical mass of people and organizations focused on the objectives and mobilized on multiple fronts with a degree of coordination rarely achieved in our collective history. But when a multi-pronged campaign is able to deploy the Total Tactic, there is no force on Earth that can stop it.

Total Tactic has a legal team to block continued attempts by power companies and their minions from perpetrating their privilege, and to put forward with vigor our CLEAR energy agenda. It operates within both administrative and legislative venues at state and federal levels. That's the Legal Offense Committee.

Total Tactic also has a Legal Defense Committee to defend in criminal court those within our critical mass who confront energy oligarchs and their minions with their bodies to prevent "business-as-usual" from steering society off the precipice. Total Tactic empowers these Energy Warriors to engage in any and all schemes and devices and maneuvers and creative stratagems with their confrontational civil disobedience, *so long as it's decent*. (Their actions *must* be decent, or else public attention gets focused on the indecency rather than the target of the action.) Then our Energy Warriors get arrested for decently confronting heinous power company behavior, and our Legal Defense Committee kicks in, complete with its Jury Project, to ensure our Energy Warriors are defended in court with top-shelf representation and that their fate is decided by peers who have enough intelligence to understand what is going on.

Total Tactic has its Education & Recruitment Committee to conduct ongoing powerful conversations throughout the community and to guide the path of those who are willing to get further involved toward our Energy Warriors, or the Legal Teams or the Media Committee, which ensures that all the action, in the courts, in the legislative halls, in the dank tunnels of the bureaucracy, and in the streets, gets the attention required to kick the whole campaign up another notch. Total Tactic operates with the understanding that everything we do today is part of the strategy that will make us stronger tomorrow.

It's not just what we are against. We have firm knowledge of how a society powered by CLEAR Energy Movement that is clean, local, efficient, affordable, equitable and reliable energy systems will function. Total Tactic therefore also has its team of engineers and technicians and business establishments that physically deploy the supply and demand side technologies of the Modern Era, and does so in conjunction with the Media Committee to ensure that *everyone* gets exposed up past their eyeballs to the ability of modern technologies to get energy right. Then maybe we can watch our oak trees grow while we wash and grind our acorns into tasty protein.

It's about power. May the power of the force be with you.

# Endnote

The energy paradigm is rapidly shifting into the Modern Era, and utility-scale energy storage technologies take a leading role in this advancement. There are many different types of storage technologies, and from the perspective of bequeathing humanity to posterity, these advancements are very encouraging. They eliminate the intermittent nature of direct wind and solar electrical generation, as well as any possible reason for new nuclear reactors. When renewable energy is no longer intermittent, it becomes dispatchable. Storage technologies make renewable energy available on demand, and renewable energy deployments with storage can then be sized to meet everything from small residential or commercial loads all the way up to the largest of industrial loads.

Battery materials, for example, identified by artificial intelligence, offer increasing efficiencies at much lower costs and without the ecological messes created by mining lithium and other rare earth metals usually associated with batteries and electronics. Green hydrogen power is coming into its own. A company called "Equatic," for example, has a new process to electrolyze sea water without producing chlorine, and that also extracts carbon dioxide, from the atmosphere. Electrolysis of water produces oxygen and hydrogen for fuel, and hydrogen fuel is now becoming green hydrogen because renewable energy is providing the electricity for the electrolysis. While these are relatively complex examples of energy storage systems, many others are remarkably simple. Masses of bricks and salts can be appropriately configured and solar heated to extremely high temperatures with mirrors and lenses, and the heated mass can then be used to produce steam for electrical generation or industrial purposes. Heavy weights of many tons can be attached by cables to electric generators above mine shafts or inside tall derricks and lifted during times of excess wind or solar generation, then lowered when it is dark and quiet.

In short, an abundance of technologies to get energy right are economically available. Now it's up to humans to deploy them equitably.

## Acknowledgments

Finally, a big and gorgeous THANK YOU to Glenn Carroll for patiently correcting all my errors, those that she could find anyway, not counting those that I refused to allow to be corrected.  So blame me for them and any others that remain.

# About the Author

George W. Crocker made a career out of intervening in a wide variety of public decisions about how to manage electric utilities, while engaging with the community education and community organizing required for successful interventions. His career includes confronting powerline construction with farmers from across West Central Minnesota beginning in 1977; intervening in Certificate of Need proceedings for power plants, numerous powerlines, and a nuclear waste dump; intervening in rulemaking proceedings to stop acid rain and reduce pollution; intervening in rate cases and electric utility planning proceedings before Public Utilities Commissions; and, leading legislative efforts to stop nuclear waste dumping in Minnesota, to promote community-based renewable energy development, and to require transmission engineers to update their planning so that the full promise of renewable energy technologies can be realized.

Mr. Crocker and his wife, Lea Foushee, founded the North American Water Office in 1982 to represent environmental and social justice interests as decisions are made regarding how electric utility services get delivered. Mr. Crocker and the North American Water Office initiated public opposition to plans of Northern States Power Company to store high-level nuclear waste in casks on Prairie Island and were on the point as this fight over nuclear waste dragged the electric utility industry of North America, kicking and screaming, into the Modern Era.

www.ingramcontent.com/pod-product-compliance
Lightning Source LLC
Chambersburg PA
CBHW021927190326
41519CB00009B/936